Transformative Strategic Thinking

Transformative Strategic Thinking

The Art of Disciplined Business Creativity

Michele Simoni, Eva Panetti, and Marco Ferretti

BEP

BUSINESS EXPERT PRESS

Leader in applied, concise business books

To our students, our greatest source of inspiration.

Description

In a time marked by rapid innovation and disruptive technologies such as artificial intelligence, compounded by unforeseen events such as the recent pandemic and pressing sustainability challenges, businesses' survival and success hinge on their ability to continuously transform.

The success stories of industry titans such as Amazon, Uber, and Airbnb underscore a vital truth: Success isn't solely about exceptional products or cutting-edge tech; it's also about innovative business models.

This book introduces the transformative strategic thinking (TST) toolkit—a creative methodology for companies eager to embrace change and explore new avenues of business model innovation. The TST toolkit blends analytical tools for dissecting existing business models with five transformational practices for experimenting with new ones.

The book concludes with real-life success stories of three entrepreneurs who navigated disrupting innovation, black swan events, and paradox management through a TST approach, effectively transforming their business models.

Diverging from traditional strategy literature, this book doesn't provide off-the-shelf formulas—it empowers you to think creatively. Through step-by-step guidance, visual collaboration tools, real-world case examples, exercises, and design tips, you'll unravel the underlying assumptions of your current business model, identify areas for improvement, and foster a creative thinking approach for experimenting with alternative models.

Designed for forward-thinking managers, daring entrepreneurs, aspiring business leaders, and ambitious start-up founders, the TST tool equips them to challenge conventional business models and design innovative ones. It's equally valuable for students and enthusiasts of business design, design thinking, and entrepreneurship.

Contents

Acknowledgments

Our work in this book is the culmination of four years of intensive research and experimentation work that has benefited the contribution of a community of academics, managers, and entrepreneurs who deserve our recognition.

A huge thanks goes to our colleagues at the Department of Management and Quantitative Studies (DISAQ) at Parthenope University. They've been a constant source of support and inspiration.

We also extend our thanks to our community of friends at MIT Sloan for their continuous support to both us and our students in countless ways. Special acknowledgment goes to Michael Cusumano, Scott Stern, and Erin Scott for their insightful conversations and invaluable feedback on our work.

A special mention goes out to Mehdi El Azhari, Milain Fayulu, Francesco Moriello, Fulvio Vinci, and Antonio Russo, the main characters of the final three chapters of this book. Their generous sharing of their entrepreneurial journeys has imbued this book with depth and purpose and has helped us crystallize its core message.

We are grateful to all the managers and entrepreneurs who graciously shared their expertise and time in our business design classes, inspiring our students with their stories and pushing them to think innovatively. Their unique perspectives have been crucial in shaping our work.

This book owes its existence to the scholars who have profoundly influenced us with their contributions.

We thank Verganti for introducing us to the concept of meaningful innovation, Chesbrough for his groundbreaking work on business model innovation, and Osterwalder and Pigneur for pioneering the use of visual collaboration tools in this field, as well as for their insights on value proposition design.

Our gratitude extends to Christensen for providing an elegant framework to navigate the disruptions we are currently witnessing and to

Johansen, Johnson, and Lewis for their illuminating insights on paradox management.

Rita Gunther McGrath's framework supporting our idea of continuous transformation, Eric Ries' eloquent explanation of the power of experimentation, and Taleb's insights about black swan events have been invaluable to us.

We want to express our gratitude to Business Expert Press and Scott Isenberg, who believed in this project and helped turn a dream into reality. We are particularly grateful to Jim Spohrer, whose suggestions and comments have greatly contributed to our work. We are also grateful to our graduate students, whose dedication and active participation in our classes have played a pivotal role in our learning and experimental journey.

Finally, to our families and loved ones, whose support and patience have been our most cherished assets, thanks.

Introduction

In the future, competition takes place not between products or companies, but between business models.
     —Gary Hamel, Professor at London Business School

The fast pace of innovation that makes firms' competitive advantages more and more temporary, the widespread diffusion of disruptive technologies such as artificial intelligence (AI), and black swan events like pandemics are reshaping the business landscape in unprecedented ways. As a result, survival and competitiveness increasingly hinge on a company's ability for continuous transformation. Consider the successes of companies such as Amazon, Uber, and Airbnb. Their triumphs weren't just about cutting-edge products or technology. In most cases, these companies' success was tied to their ability to find alternative ways to create and capture value. Business model logic (BML) describes the assumptions about how a company produces value for customers and appropriates part of it. More specifically, the definition of a business model is built upon a consistent and cohesive logic based on a set of primarily hidden assumptions about different aspects of the value creation process that ultimately legitimizes the model. Fifteen years ago, if someone had told us that we could find value in sleeping at some strangers' place to the extent that we would pay for it, we would have probably just laughed. However, a company such as Airbnb was able to design a business model that not only challenged a deeply ingrained childhood assumption—"do not sleep at strangers' place"—but made it a desirable choice. The crux of business model innovation lies in disrupting the existing BML by recognizing and challenging its main assumptions. Recent years have demonstrated that in most industries, driving forces such as globalization, digitalization, and commoditization are accelerating product obsolescence, making it harder for big companies to stay ahead of the competition.

Moreover, the swift pace of innovation is blurring the traditional boundaries between industries. As a result, companies find themselves competing in dynamic environments where both the nature of competitors and the rules of the game are in a constant state of flux. The iconic downfall of Blockbuster due to the advent of Netflix's streaming platforms is a clear example of how business myopia about change can be detrimental. Blockbuster regarded Netflix as a niche for web services' early adopters and stuck to its business logic based on offline DVD rental. Blockbuster clung to its traditional DVD-centered business model, dismissing Netflix's pioneering online services as catering only to early adopters. It wasn't until Netflix successfully converted Blockbuster's original core clientele into their own customers that Blockbuster attempted to adapt, launching Blockbuster Online in 2004. However, by then, it was too late; Netflix had already solidified its position in the streaming market. Just five years later, Blockbuster filed for bankruptcy. We have learned from recent successful (and unsuccessful) stories that real success depends on the level of firms' openness to change and their capacity to challenge established business models, seeking fresh avenues to deliver value. Typically, the inertia to business model innovation is tied to large companies' resistance to change and their slow and complex decision-making process steeped in extensive planning to avoid the unexpected. Recent history is replete with cases of large firms failing due to their aversion to change and an overestimation of their enduring competitive advantage. Yet, a frequently underestimated obstacle to business model innovation lies in the limited mindset of individual entrepreneurs and managers, which hinders them from going beyond their current business logic and questioning their assumptions. The prevailing managerial approach, centered on planning and execution, often hinders the creativity and experimentation needed for disruptive business model innovation. To address this, we propose adopting a disciplined creative thinking approach: transformative strategic thinking (TST). This approach guides the process through distinct steps: recognizing the current logic design, challenging fundamental assumptions, transforming elements of the business logic, ensuring consistency, and, ultimately, experimenting with the new business model.

The TST tool

In this book, we present the TST tool to help companies disrupt themselves and experiment with alternative business model transformations.

The TST is a tool that can guide companies in:

1. Recognizing the assumptions that underpin their current business model.
2. Experimenting with alternative BML transformations.
3. Recreating a new consistent BML.

For these purposes, the TST provides a combination of:

- Analytical tools: The TST elements—to recognize the assumptions of the current business model;
- Transformational tools: The TST practices—to play with the current assumptions and experiment with new business models to ultimately recreate a new consistent BML.

The TST Elements

The BML represents a set of hypotheses/assumptions about how a company creates value for its customers and generates revenues.

First, we suggest that the BML can be broken down into five main elements that we consider particularly effective in identifying the BML's assumptions (Figure I.1):

1. Meaning: Why do people love a specific product or service?
2. Experiential Performance: Which are the relevant aspects of the customer experience?
3. Resources: What are the key resources, and who controls them?
4. Roles: What are the key activities, and who is accountable for them?
5. Value Equation: What benefits does the customer perceive in a specific product or service, and what efforts are required to attain those benefits?

Analyzing the five elements allows a complete understanding of the business model's current assumptions. The book provides a step-by-step guide to exploring each element through frameworks and design tips, which will help unveil the most profound assumptions of the value

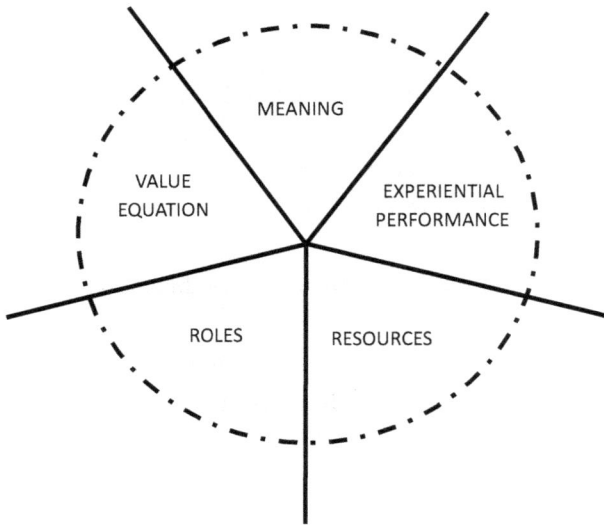

Figure I.1 The TST elements

creation process. A deep understanding of the current business model is a crucial prerequisite for its transformation.

The TST Practices

Secondly, the aforementioned elements can be easily transformed by leveraging their subdimensions. To this aim, we propose a transformational practice for each element—the Five S' Framework (Figure I.2):

1. Shaping: Rethink the meaning.
2. Stretching: Emphasize or de-emphasize certain aspects of the experience.
3. Sharing: Modify the essential resources and their control regime.
4. Switching: Change the flow of critical activities and define new roles.
5. Swapping: Redefine the value equation.

These practices can help to unlock managers' and entrepreneurs' creativity and develop an experimental mindset that will challenge the assumptions of their current business models and redesign the business according to new hypotheses. By using one of those five practices, the

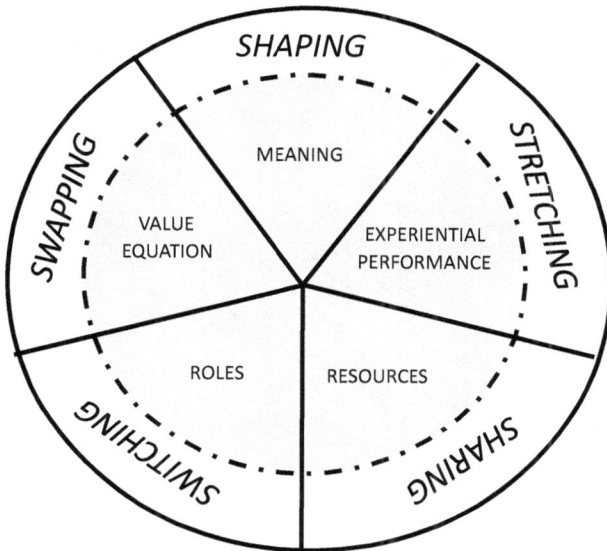

Figure I.2 The TST practices

idea is to trigger a BML transformation, starting by exploring the transformation of one single element and verifying how the other elements
can be realigned to recreate a new consistent BML, that is, the domino
effect. In fact, by practicing the method, you will see that the transformation of just one of the five elements opens the path to multiple options
to trigger a cascade transformation of the other pieces of the business
logic. What's more—you can reiterate the transformation process until
you don't find a new BML that is consistent and helpful for new business
experimentations.

The first five chapters of this book are dedicated to guiding the readers
to use the five practices, including the discussion of real-world examples
of business model transformations, frameworks, and exercises.

The TST Challenge

The book's last three chapters illustrate a few managerial/entrepreneur-
ial challenges that typically affect companies' current logic of value
creation.

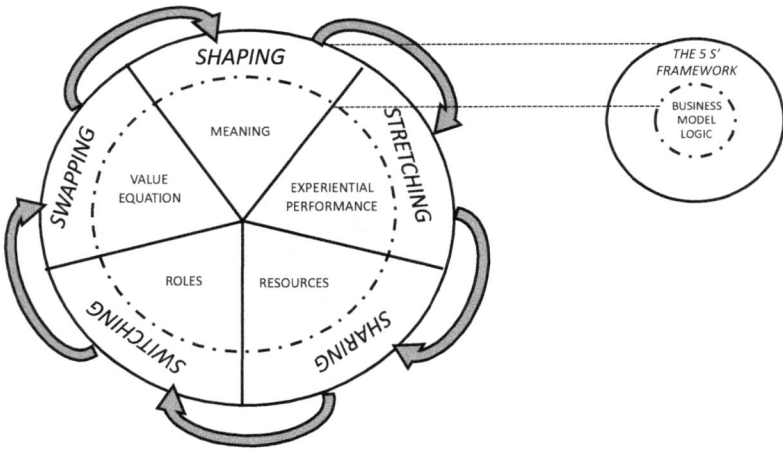

Figure I.3 The domino effect

In particular, we suggest that the TST can help cope with change and gain back competitiveness in three main scenarios:

1. Black swan events: A black swan is a rare, unexpected event with massive consequences. Black swans can positively or negatively affect how a market or industry functions. The TST tool can be used to identify which element(s) of the BML is most negatively affected by the black swan and eventually operate a transformation of the whole business model by realigning the elements with the ones showing the highest upside potential.

2. Disruptive innovation: An innovation that displaces an established technology. Initially appealing to a limited audience, it may need more refinement for many years and affect how a market or industry functions in the long term. The TST tool can identify/experiment with the impact on the BML—from a transformative perspective—deriving from the evolution of a new (potentially disruptive) technology.

3. Paradox management: A strategy to pursue simultaneously two conflicting goals (i.e., social and profit). The tool can be used to identify alternative BMLs responding to both goals and eventually mix the elements of the two antithetical business models to maximize value creation.

To cope with these challenges, the TST tool can help rethink the business model in light of the changes resulting from these scenarios.

Who Should Read This Book?

The book is designed for managers and entrepreneurs who want to drive change in their organizations. It is also for start-uppers who intend to launch a new project by challenging existing business models in a specific industry or arena. Finally, the book targets students and those interested in business design, design thinking, or entrepreneurship. Business cases, visual collaboration tools, and exercises will help the readers start practicing with the TST tool and become familiar with the different transformational practices.

CHAPTER 1

Shaping the Meaning

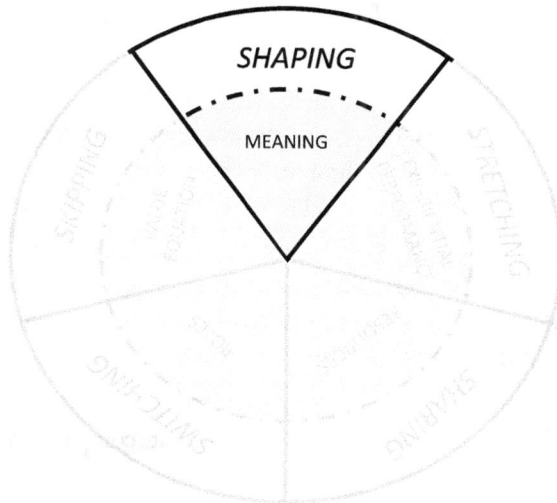

Figure 1.1 Shaping the meaning

What Will You Learn?

You will:

- Understand which aspects define the meaning of a Business Model Logic (BML).
- Learn how to analyze the meaning in a BML.
- Learn how to design the meaning in a BML practically.
- Understand how to trigger a BML transformation by shaping the meaning.
- Understand the implications of shaping the meaning in a BML from real-world business examples (Figure 1.1).

Element #1 the Meaning: A Product Love Story

One thing is to improve a product or to solve a problem better. Another thing is to design an experience that people truly love.
—Roberto Verganti, 2016

The experience related to the acquisition of a product or service concerns all those intangible aspects in the consumption process that go beyond their mere functionality, including not only the context of usage of the product or the delivery of the service but also the values and emotions that a specific offering evokes in the customer perception. The experience explains not how a product/service works and serves customers' needs but *why* customers need a particular product/service. In our current world, new ideas are abundant, and to create value, businesses should give customers something they are passionate about, something they *love*. If something is loved by the people who consume it, business value will follow. Indeed, the secret behind many successful companies lies in designing *delightful experiences* rather than efficient solutions. Consider Nest Labs, the thermostat company now under Google's umbrella, known as Google Nest. Rather than focusing solely on creating more advanced programmable thermostats, the company recognized that most people don't enjoy spending time programming home appliances. In response, Nest took a different approach and engineered a thermostat that learns the household's habits and adjusts the temperature accordingly. This innovative design transformed the way we interact with our home climate control systems. Hence, designing an experience that people genuinely love becomes crucial for businesses. But why do people love an experience that a particular product/service enables? Why do people purchase a specific service/product over another one? These questions underlie the first element of the Business Model Logic (BML): the *meaning*. Quoting Irvin D. Yalom, an existential psychiatrist, "*We are meaning-seeking creatures*," and the reason we are induced to buy a product over another with similar characteristics goes far beyond the simple functionality that certain products embed. Indeed, in a world *overcrowded with ideas, absolute value is defined as what is meaningful, which is necessary to make a difference nowadays.*

Think about Moleskine, the famous brand of essential smooth-cover notebooks. With their iconic black carnet, the Italian notebook manufacturer has increased its revenues by 40 percent over the past two years (Statista, 2023).[*] This is an outstanding result considering the spread diffusion of digital devices and the wide availability of cheaper alternatives in the staid stationery market. The *Moleskine Phenomenon* is primarily explained by the company's ability to sell an *extremely ordinary* product as an object of desire or even a lifestyle tool. Imbuing the meaning of Moleskine with fascinating storytelling about how Picasso, Hemingway, or Van Gogh used to sketch and draft their masterpieces on the classic black notebook gave a unique meaning to the experience provided by the product. Most people love Moleskine since owning its products makes them feel part of a community. A community of *knowledge workers* as artists, designers, architects, and even lawyers and engineers, all having in common the willingness to maintain a physical experience with their idea generation process—or more simply note-taking activities—and of being recognized not so much for their level of income but rather by their level of education. This is how Moleskine has nurtured a new direction and provided a notebook with a unique meaning. Hence, defining the meaning means identifying the reason why people *love* (and buy) a specific product/service and its relevance/role in the customer's consumption system. In essence, it's crucial to grasp how a product or service seamlessly integrates into a person's array of consumption activities. In fact, a product's or service's consumption process is seldom isolated. More often than not, it is complemented by one or several other experiences. For example, you could buy an expensive set of luxurious chopsticks because you are a huge sushi lover or a kitchen design enthusiast with a thing for Japanese culture and lifestyle. Or, you might be willing to invest a fortune in a handcrafted ebony bookshelf just for the pleasure of utterly organizing your old books collection inherited from your long-lost grandfather, even if you are not exactly a bookworm. Hence, a fondness for the

---

[*]Statista is a German online platform for statistics, which makes data collected by market and opinion research institutes and data derived from the economic sector.

Asian lifestyle and the need to keep a loved one's memory alive may significantly emphasize the role played by a particular experience in the user consumption system.

Wrap-Up Questions

To sum up, the meaning of the BML can be defined by two fundamental questions:

1. Why do people buy/love an experience provided by a specific product/service?
2. How relevant is an experience provided by the product/service in customers' consumption system?

Warm-Up Task

1. Pick a successful product or service that you know well. Name at least three reasons why you think people love the experience the product or service provides.

Brand/Product:_____

1._____
2._____
3._____
4._____
5._____

2. Think about the product/service that you mentioned; name at least three consumption activities that make it relevant in a customer's consumption system.

1._____
2._____
3._____
4._____
5._____

Understanding the Meaning

As we noted in the case of the stationary market, people buy and love a specific value offering depending on factors beyond their mere functionality.

People buy and love the experience provided by Moleskine because it is evocative of a certain status, that is, the feeling of belonging to the knowledge workers community (the *reason why*), which, in turn, contributes to making a relevant consumption activity—such as taking notes while working or traveling—more *meaningful* by remarking a particular lifestyle (relevance/role in the consumption activities).

Therefore, the reason why people *love* an experience provided by a specific product/service and its relevance/role in the customer's consumption system can be defined by three dimensions, that is, the product/service end-use, usage context, and symbolic significance, which altogether define the BML's meaning.

Specifically, to analyze and design a product or service *meaning,* use an essential analytic tool to break down the meaning's analysis in three easy steps:

- **Step 1. Define the End-Use:** To understand on which occasions and to what purposes the experience related to a particular product/service is considered relevant.
- **Step 2. Delimit the Usage Context:** To define in association to which other experiences or within which different experiences the product/service is used.
- **Step 3. Unveil the Symbolic Significance:** To understand which values and feelings the experience related to the consumption of a particular product/service evokes.

Combining the end-use with the delimitation of the usage context and the definition of the symbolic significance defines the meaning of a specific experience related to a particular product/service.

These subdimensions contribute to understanding and identifying the hidden assumptions underlying the meaning by providing a comprehensive view of why people love a specific product or service (Figure 1.2).

MEANING		
END-USE	**USAGE CONTEXT**	**SYMBOLIC SIGNIFICANCE**
For which purposes do people use the product/service?	In association with which other experiences the product/service is seen as relevant?	What feelings and emotions does the product/service evoke?
Clients use .... for ...	Clients use ... in/with ...	Clients use ... to feel ...
People love .... because		

Figure 1.2 Meaning subdimensions

Step 1. Define the End-Use

The *meaning end-use* refers to the variety of occasions when the experience associated with a specific product/service is seen as relevant. You can define this subdimension by answering questions such as:

- When does the experience provided by a product/service occur?
- On which specific occasions do people see the experience provided by the product/service as relevant?
- For which purposes do people pursue the experience provided by the product/service?

Let's take *Compasses Magazine*, an architecture and design magazine issued every four months with a geographical focus on the Middle East. In this case, the *meaning end-use* would be (i) gaining insight into design and architecture and being more acknowledged about that domain in the specific Middle East context. In the alternative, *meaning end-use* can refer to (ii) finding exotic inspiration for their home interiors. Finally, the *meaning end-use* can be (iii) discovering new places they have not visited yet, driven by the high-quality level of the pictures in the magazine (Figure 1.3).

Design Tips

Define a *meaning end-use* by simply answering the question: "In which occasions/to what purpose is the experience provided by the product/service seen as relevant?" For example: "The user buys *Compasses Magazine* when he/she wants to find exotic inspiration."

Step 2. Delimit the Usage Context

A second issue we should define is the *meaning usage context*, the actual conditions under which an experience related to the consumption of a given item or service takes place or will unfold in an ordinary customer's situation. In other words, you should visualize and define typical conditions in which your target customers would use your value offering, including the complementary products, services, or experiences that concur with its consumption. If we go back to *Compasses Magazine*, we can imagine people reading the magazine while traveling for business, maybe on a leather-covered armchair while sipping a glass of Prosecco. Or, we can imagine an architect carefully positioning the magazine on the coffee table in their office as a signal of expertise for their clients. By picturing the context in which the product or service is likely to be used, it will be easier to understand the intangible aspects of the experience that make the product loved by customers (Figure 1.3).

Design Tips

Define a *meaning usage context* by simply answering the question: In association with which other types of experiences is the offering typically used? For example: "The user buys *Compasses Magazine* when he/she travels business class."

Step 3. Unveil the Symbolic Significance

The last step in defining the meaning is to identify the *meaning symbolic significance*, the evocative representation of the offering in the customer's mind. This consists of determining the sensemaking process behind customers' purchasing behavior by trying to understand what the offering represents to the customer, including the concepts and values evoked by it. In the case of *Compasses Magazine* focus on Middle Eastern architecture and design, customers may associate the magazine with a sense of belonging to an international elite, maybe with a luxurious lifestyle that people dream of. Understanding the *meaning symbolic significance* will help gain insight into what makes the experience of a particular product or service more or less remarkable compared to similar ones (Figure 1.3).

Design Tips

Define a *meaning symbolic significance* by answering the questions; "What does the product/service represent for the customer?" and "Which concepts and values does the product or service evoke?" For example: "With *Compasses Magazine*, the user can feel part of an international community."

MEANING		
END-USE	**USAGE CONTEXT**	**SYMBOLIC SIGNIFICANCE**
For which purposes do people use the product/service?	In association with which other experiences the product/service is seen as relevant?	What feelings and emotions does the product/service evoke?
Clients use **Compasses** for/when ...	Clients use **Compasses** in/with ...	Clients use **Compasses** to feel ...
learning about design & architecture finding inspiration for their home	business travels comfortable/relaxing settings	part of an international community luxury
discovering new places	office decorations demonstrating expertise	sophisticated
People love Compasses because *it's a stylish way to learn and explore*		

Figure 1.3 Compasses magazine meaning

So What?

In summary, the meaning can be defined by three main subdimensions: end-use, usage context, and symbolic significance. A deep understanding of the purposes that make the offering valuable, the consumption context and ecosystem in which the offering is typically used, and the intangible aspects that make the product/service unique allow us to define better why people love a particular product/service.

TST Challenge

Analyze and report in the following diagram the key subdimensions of the meaning of the following business: Nespresso coffee-making system.[†] Then, synthesize the three subdimensions to define the meaning. Use the templates provided as follows (Figure 1.4).

MEANING		
END-USE	**USAGE CONTEXT**	**SYMBOLIC SIGNIFICANCE**
For which purposes did people use the product/service?	In association with which other experiences the product/service is seen as relevant?	What feelings and emotions does the product/service evoke?
Clients use Nespresso for ...	Clients use Nespresso in/with ...	Clients use Nespresso to feel ...

People love Nespresso because ....

Figure 1.4 Meaning worksheet

[†]Nespresso is a globally renowned coffee company known for its premium coffee machines and capsules. Established by Nestlé, it specializes in providing convenient and high-quality coffee experiences to consumers. Nespresso has carved a niche in the market for those seeking a refined and smooth coffee brewing experience. www.nespresso.com/it/en/.

TST Practice #1 Transforming the Business Model Logic by Shaping the Meaning

The transformational practice of the meaning is *shaping*, which refers to the process of rethinking the meaning. Simply put, *shaping the meaning* means transforming the current reason why people love or buy a product into a new reason to buy or adopt a product, a service, a platform, or whatever is at the core of a business model. After having identified the meaning of three subdimensions, that is, end-use, usage context, and symbolic significance in your product or service BML (see Step 1, Step 2, and Step 3 in the previous section), you can start thinking about how the original meaning can be rethought by changing one or more meaning subdimensions. This means that the meaning can be rethought in three different ways.

Shaping by Repurposing the Meaning End-Use

First, you can rethink the meaning by changing the *end-use*. Think about the U.S.-based company Yankee Candle: "the world's best-loved candle." With more than 500 company-owned retail stores and over 19,000 authorized retailers in the United States and 24 countries worldwide, the company has been one of the world's best-known and bestselling brands in the candle business for the last 45 years. But what is so special about Yankee Candles? Which innovation did the company introduce to be so successful? The main reason behind Yankee Candle's success lay in the firm's ability to convey a new *meaning end-use* to a product of large consumption in a declining stage of its life cycle. Indeed, while looking at the candle's original meaning (before Yankee Candle went on the market but later than the advent of electricity), people bought candles for *emergency* reasons. The candle was the typical item to be purchased and stored in a drawer just in case…. The case was generally a shortage of electricity or a blackout in the household.

Consequently, no matter whether the candle was fancily designed or embellished, the dominant meaning was traceable to its pure function of lightning. Over time, candles became less and less used due to the widespread diffusion of battery-powered devices—such as torches

—that could replace the candles' emergency lighting function much more efficiently. However, when the original emergency *reason* to buy a candle started to fade away, Yankee Candle redesigned the business logic model by defining a new *meaning* for candles and giving people a new *reason* to buy them. And what is the new reason? Well, with over 150 fragrances of different sizes and colors, Yankee Candles suggested that candles could be used to create a friendly and pleasant atmosphere or decorate an interior on special occasions, such as for romantic dates or parties. Since then, the candle market has grown significantly, and the manufacturers have modified the product to fit this new meaning, for example, in colors, designs, scents, and so on.

In this case, the meaning of candles has been shaped by repurposing the *meaning end-use* from an item used for lightening (eventually in case of emergency) to decorating and creating an atmosphere (Figure 1.5).

Shaping by Moving the Meaning Usage Context

As a second option to shape and rethink the meaning, you could leverage the *meaning usage context*, changing the current circumstances in which customers typically use a given item or service. Think about The North Face, the famous sportswear brand that started in the late 1960s as a climbing equipment retail store in North Beach, San Francisco.

For years, the brand has been targeting a niche market of adventurers by providing good quality rock climbing and camping equipment. The iconic coats—the Mountain Gore-Tex jacket and the Mountain Light jacket—were initially designed for extreme skiwear, to the extent that the company was asked to create exclusive polar clothing for the international Trans-Antarctica Expedition in the 1990s. For decades, the brand had a clear understanding of the *meaning usage context* of its products. People associated The North Face products with exploration, adventure, and extreme outdoor activities. However, after a corporate crisis, the company changed its strategy by expanding its market beyond outdoor enthusiasts. Since the 2000s, The North Face started to be

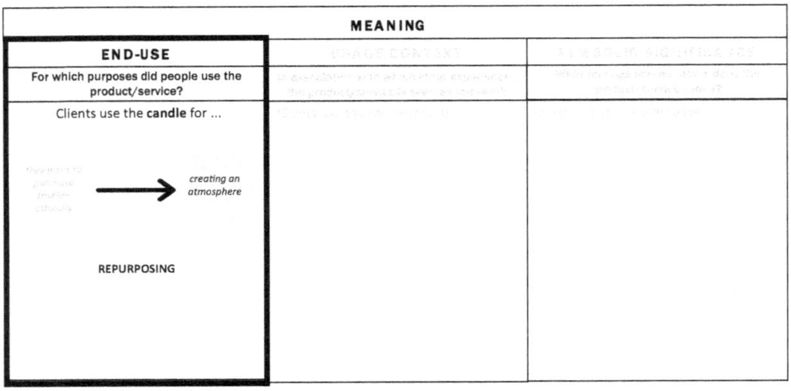

MEANING		
END-USE		
For which purposes did people use the product/service?		
Clients use the **candle** for ...		
→ creating an atmosphere		
REPURPOSING		

Figure 1.5 Shaping by repurposing the meaning

regarded as a streetwear style brand, thanks to the rise of the athleisure trend, athletic apparel that people can wear in nonathletic settings.

Indeed, The North Face launched several capsule collections in the last years in collaboration with high-end fashion brands such as Supreme and Gucci. The North Face customers increasingly wore the brand products in various social situations unrelated to sports and adventures. You can see teenagers wearing their The North Face coats to go to school and emulate their rap idols' style, or it-girls sporting their The North Face x Gucci co-branded jackets while sipping a Spritz in Piazza Duomo in Milan for their weekly aperitivo. In this case, the brand's meaning has been *shaped by moving the meaning usage context*— from a product used in exploration, adventure, and outdoor activities— to a product line used in casual and social occasions (Figure 1.6).

Shaping by Changing the Meaning Symbolic Significance

As a third option, you could change the *symbolic significance* assigned by customers to a specific product or service to shape and rethink the meaning. Let's take an example in the industry of social media platforms, such as Facebook. Initially, the platform was conceived to find long-lost friends from college and catch up with them. The *symbolic significance* was associated with evoking the good old times and feeling the comfort of still being part of a community of people despite physical

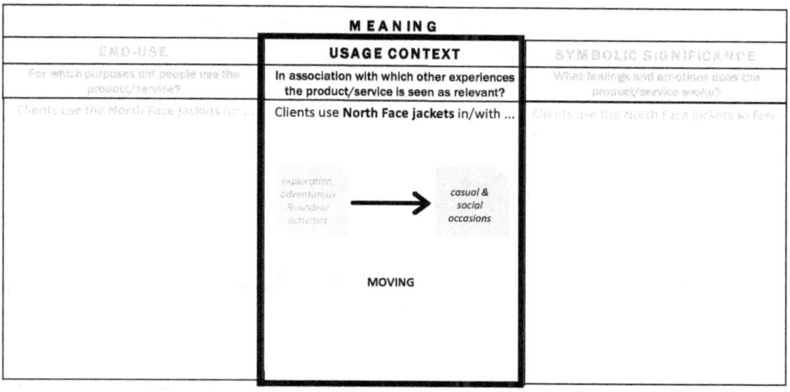

MEANING		
END-USE	USAGE CONTEXT	SYMBOLIC SIGNIFICANCE
For which purposes did people use the product/service?	In association with which other experiences the product/service is seen as relevant?	What feelings and emotions does the product/service evoke?
Clients use the North Face jackets for ...	Clients use **North Face jackets** in/with ...	Clients use the North Face jackets to feel ...
	exploration adventurous &outdoor activities → casual & social occasions	
	MOVING	

Figure 1.6 Shaping by moving the meaning usage context

distance or different lifestyles. The initial concept behind Facebook was an instant messaging system meeting peoples' need for interaction and networking. The initial platform—*The Facebook*—launched in 2004, allowing users to have a personal profile to upload photos, share their interests, and connect with others. But after a while, with the introduction of *likes*, *comments*, and *pokes*, the users were pushed to share more details about their lifestyle—from their pet's birthday to the pictures of their weekend at the beach. Many people started to develop a psychological addiction to the *likes* from their community of virtual friends. They began to post more instead of directly communicating with friends. Since then, the platform started to have a different symbolic

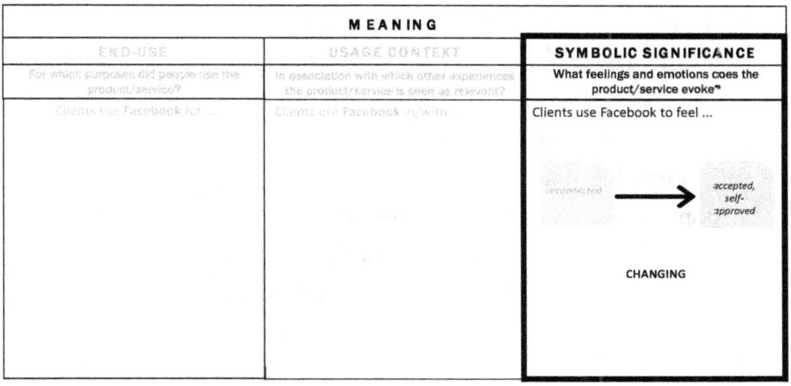

MEANING		
END-USE	USAGE CONTEXT	SYMBOLIC SIGNIFICANCE
For which purposes did people use the product/service?	In association with which other experiences the product/service is seen as relevant?	What feelings and emotions does the product/service evoke*
Clients use Facebook for ...	Clients use Facebook in/with ...	Clients use Facebook to feel ...
		reconnected → accepted, self-approved
		CHANGING

Figure 1.7 Shaping by changing the symbolic significance

significance to people, from a tool to feel connected with others to a device to feel social acceptance, self-approval, or even an influence on others (Figure 1.7).

Key Takeaways

To sum up, to transform the BML by shaping, you can rethink the meaning by leveraging one or more of its three subdimensions. Specifically, the meaning can be shaped by:

1. Repurposing the meaning end-use of the original BML.
2. Moving the meaning usage context of the original BML.
3. Changing the meaning symbolic significance of the original BML.

   You can rethink and redefine the original meaning by performing one of the three operations. This will trigger a transformation of the whole BML of your value offering.

Business Case Example

Shaping the Meaning of Wristwatches: The Apple Smart Watch:
Released in April 2015, the Apple Watch was the first new Apple device to be launched during the leadership of Tim Cook. The Apple Watch was also the first new category of product to be developed after the iPad, allowing the company to make its foray into wearable technology. The Apple Watch was designed to integrate the iOS system and connect to other iOS users' devices. It allowed them to check notifications, make calls, send texts, and use supported third-party applications explicitly designed for the wrist. Even if the Apple Watch has not been living up to expectations in terms of sales and popularity in the mass market, as it has not proven to be as indispensable as the iPhone or even as profitable as the Mac or the iPad, it is undeniable that it was designed to be a game-changing device that transformed the meaning of the traditional wristwatch

(Continued)

(Continued)

into a completely new one. Wristwatches were introduced in the nineteenth century. They were first worn chiefly by military men to replace pocket watches, less practical for synchronizing maneuvers during battles or while mounting on a horse. Later on, with the introduction of electric-powered wristwatches, the wristwatch reached the mass market and became little by little a product to check the time and a fashion accessory. The smartwatch rethought the meaning of the wristwatch as "a product to check the time and embellish your outfit" by providing users with a new reason to buy a wristwatch. A smartwatch is a computer worn on the wrist, having the functionalities of a mobile phone, music player, digital assistant, and even health care device in some of their newest versions. This changed the wristwatch's meaning end-use from mere timekeeping to that of bridging the divide between our digital existence and physical pursuits (i.e., answering phone calls, texts, checking physical activity, etc.). But it also changed the meaning usage context from a product used for special occasions (in the case of precious watches) to something used in your everyday life in association with other devices such as the iPhone. Finally, the Apple Watch presents a different symbolic significance, from an item evoking a timeless elegance to a product evoking the feeling of being constantly connected and up-to-date. The smartwatch allows people not to interrupt their connectivity, ensuring that even during activities like rigorous physical training, the flow of digital interactions remains uninterrupted. Apple's foray into this space signifies more than just a product; it embodies a paradigm shift in our perception of wristwatches, setting a new standard for wearable technologies.

Chapter Overview

In this chapter, we defined the first element of the Business Model Logic (BML): the *meaning*; that is the reason why people love (and buy) a product, and its relevance in the customer's consumption system.

Meaning can be analyzed and designed by a three-step process in which you define the meaning end-use, usage context, and, finally, the symbolic significance. Finally, we illustrated the first BML transformational practice, shaping. A shaping practice can be defined as rethinking and redesigning BML by changing one or more of the meaning subdimensions.

CHAPTER 2

Stretching the Experiential Performance

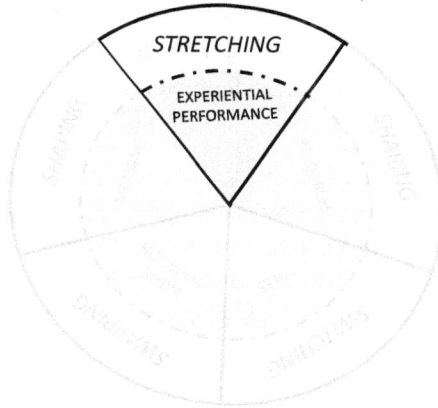

Figure 2.1 Stretching the experiential performance

What Will You Learn?

You will:

- Understand which aspects define the experiential performance (EP) in a Business Model Logic (BML).
- Learn how to analyze the EP in a BML.
- Learn how to design the EP in a BML practically.
- Understand how to trigger a BML transformation by stretching the EP.
- Understand the implications of stretching the EP in a BML from real-world business examples (Figure 2.1).

Element #2 the Experiential Performance: Creating a Memorable Customer Experience

You can't transform something you don't understand. If you don't know and understand the current state of the customer experience, how can you design the desired future state?

—Annette Franz, founder and chief experience officer of CX
Journey Inc.

Transforming a customer experience requires a deep understanding of its current state. Annette Franz, a renowned authority in customer experience, emphasizes this crucial foundation. To embark on a redesign journey, one must first grasp the intricacies of the existing customer experience. This comprehension lays the groundwork for envisioning the desired future state. Managers, therefore, need to address pivotal questions: What elements of the customer experience truly drive value? How should these aspects be prioritized? These questions serve as the cornerstone of the second element of the BML, specifically, the Experiential Performance (EP). Clare Muscutt, a distinguished figure in customer experience entrepreneurship, said, *"Building a good customer experience does not happen by accident. It happens by design."* This sentiment highlights the deliberate effort needed to provide excellent customer experiences. Crucially, this requires a thorough examination and breakdown of the customer experience related to a certain product or service. This allows organizations to choose which aspects of the experience should be prioritized and improved, eventually driving innovation. Think about Starbucks, the world-renowned coffee shop chain with over 19,000 locations in 58 countries, which has become a leader in the retail coffee industry. As we all know, Starbucks's *EP* is not just about serving good coffee. In fact, besides the quality of the coffee, the company has historically focused on other experiential factors such as atmosphere, customer service, and food and drink selection. Starbucks's emphasis on key facets of the customer experience, and subsequently the crafting of innovative *EP*, is founded on the transformative process of redefining the meaning (as explored in Chapter 1) of the coffee shop: evolving it from a mere transactional space for purchasing coffee into a welcoming environment where people can savor a high-quality cup of coffee while indulging in various activities and social interactions. By leveraging specific aspects of the *EP*, such as the *location*, Starbucks ingeniously cultivated a welcoming and cozy environment where customers could work, have business meetings, lounge with friends, or read a book. As a result, Starbucks profoundly shifted the global perspective on coffee shops, establishing them as *third places* beyond the realms of home and office—a space where individuals gather, connect, and seamlessly carry out their daily routines. Simon Sinek, the author of *Start With Why* (2009), wrote: "*Starbucks was founded around the experience and the environment of their stores. Starbucks was about a space with comfortable chairs, lots of power outlets, tables and desks at which we could work, and the option to spend as much time in their stores as we wanted without any pressure to buy. The coffee was incidental.*" This idea of the coffee shop as a *third place* explains how Starbucks has redesigned the *EP* of the coffee shop by imagining a brand new customer experience. If the first issue of performance relates to identifying relevant aspects of the customer experience, the second issue pertains to *prioritizing* the relevant elements. Let's consider the *EP* of a Michelin-star restaurant, for example. You will surely notice that consumers are willing to wait a long time between courses and the time spent listening to never-ending explanations about the extraction of the Himalayan root that was used to season their gourmet salad. This is because *service speed* is not vital to the customer experience. Instead, this type of service might prioritize, for example, *Instagram-worthy* plating allowing customers to share their fancy experience on social media in real-time. The emphasis placed to certain aspects of the customer experience over others contributes to defining the *EP*.

Wrap-Up Questions

In summary, the EP of a BML can be defined by addressing two fundamental questions:

1. Which aspects of customer experience are relevant in the process of value creation?
2. How are these aspects hierarchically prioritized?

Warm-Up Task

1. Select a successful product or service that you are familiar with. List up to five characteristics that define the customer experience related to the consumption of this product/service.

Brand/Product:_____

1._____
2._____
3._____
4._____
5._____

2. What are the key characteristics you've identified as most important in the overall customer experience, and how would you prioritize them? List them below in order of importance (from most critical to least significant).

1._____
2._____
3._____
4._____
5._____

Understanding the Experiential Performance

As we noted in the case of the food business industry, the user experience can be designed by leveraging several dimensions, including tangible factors, such as food quality, price, and setting, and intangible factors, such as personnel expertise or atmosphere. To analyze and design a product or service *EP*, use an essential analytic tool to break down the EP design process into three easy steps:

- **Step 1. List the Experiential Building Blocks (EBBs)** to recognize the various opportunities and options involved in the customer experience.
- **Step 2. Identify the Experiential Benchmarks (EBKs)** to understand how your product/service provides more or less value than similar offerings.
- **Step 3. Qualify the Experiential Building Blocks (EQ) for each Experiential Benchmark** to define how the different opportunities and options involved in the customer experience are supported and differentiated.
  - o The combination of the EBBs with the corresponding experiential quality (EQ) and EBK defines EP (EBB +EQ + EBK = EP).

These subdimensions help understanding and uncovering the implicit assumptions that underlie *EP*. They offer a comprehensive view of the key aspects of the customer experience (Figure 2.2).

Step 1. List the Experiential Building Blocks

An EBB encompasses the array of options and opportunities a particular product or service offers, enhancing the overall customer experience. Defining this subdimension involves addressing pivotal questions:

EXPERIENTIAL PERFORMANCE		
EXPERIENTIAL BUILDING BLOCKS (EBB)	EXPERIENTIAL QUALITY (EQ)	EXPERIENTIAL BENCHMARK (EBK)
What are the relevant aspects of the customer experience?	In which way do these aspects create more value?	Compared to what substitute/similar experiences?
With ... the user can	How?	Differently from ....

Figure 2.2 Experiential performance subdimension

- What are the relevant aspects of the customer experience?
- What opportunities does the offering provide the customer with?

Let's take *Compasses Magazine*, an architecture and design magazine issued every four months with a geographical focus on the Middle East, featuring editorials from world-renowned architects and breathtaking shots by excellent international photographers. The magazine is available both online and in hard copy. The *Compasses EBBs* can refer to (i) embarking on virtual architectural journeys worldwide and (ii) staying updated on emerging trends in home decoration from the comfort of your own space (Figure 2.3).

Design Tips

Define an EBB by using the sentence: "With (name of the firm/ product/service) the user can ...." For example: "With *Compasses Magazine*, the user can take virtual architectural tours worldwide."

Step 2. Find the Experiential Benchmark

The second step in defining *EP* is identifying the EBK. This consists of considering various options and possibilities in light of similar

EXPERIENTIAL PERFORMANCE		
EXPERIENTIAL BUILDING BLOCKS (EBB)	EXPERIENTIAL QUALITY (EQ)	EXPERIENTIAL BENCHMARK (EBK)
What are the relevant aspects of the customer experience?	In which way do these aspects create more value?	Compared to what substitute/similar experiences?
With **Compasses** the user can	How?	Differently from ....
TAKE VIRTUAL ARCHITECTURAL JOURNEYS WORLDWIDE	In a more ACCESSIBLE way	TRAVELS
LEARN ABOUT ARCHITECTURE AND DEISGN	In a more ECOFRIENDLY way In a more ACCESSIBLE way	PAPER MAGAZINES
STAYING UPDATED ON EMERGING TRENDS IN HOME DECORATION	In a CHEAPER way	CONFERENCES/WORKSHOPS

Figure 2.3 Compasses magazine experiential performance

experiences to establish a reference point for our EBBs. An EBK does not only refer to similar products or services but also to offerings that provide a similar experience to the customer, even if these are entirely different products or services. For example, look at one of the *Compasses Magazine*'s EBB: "With *Compasses Magazine*, the user can gain knowledge about architecture and design." We realize this is an opportunity that can be provided to customers through products other than magazines, such as books and websites, and even services, such as specialized workshops or conferences. Attending an architecture and design workshop or reading an architecture and design magazine will leave the customer feeling more knowledgeable. Two completely different types of offerings—workshop vs magazine—can deliver comparable experiences (Figure 2.3).

Design Tips

Once you define your EBK for a specific EBB, leave a space between them. This will give you time to reflect on how the EBB in your current EP provides a superior (or inferior) value compared to the specific EBK.

Step 3. Qualify the Experiential Building Block

Once we have identified the list of EBBs provided by a specific value offering and the corresponding competing experiences (EBK), we define the EQ. The EQ describes in which way each EBB creates more value compared to similar or substitute offerings in the market (EBK). We can determine the EQ by identifying an adjective/adverb that qualifies the EBB. Going back to the *Compasses Magazine* example, the digital format's availability would make learning about architecture and design (EBB) *more accessible* or *more eco-friendly* when compared with magazines that only issue paper magazines.

Of course, reading a magazine requires much less effort in terms of time and money, while attending a workshop requires traveling to the location, paying a fee, active listening, and so on. The point is to show how the reported EBB provides a superior value (Figure 2.3).

Design Tips

Define the EQ by adding an adjective or an adverbial phrase to the EBB phrasing. For example: "With *Compasses Magazine*, the user can stay updated on emerging trends in home decoration (EBB) more sustainably (EQ) than paper magazine (EBK)." You can find more EQs for the same EBB, and the same EQ can refer to more EBKs.

So What?

Defining the EBBs, the EQ, and the EBK contributes to future considerations regarding which aspects of EP are relevant (or irrelevant) in making the user experience valuable. These considerations then will guide stretching transformation processes by suggesting which EBBs are worth emphasizing (because they make the whole experience unique compared to similar experiences) and which elements could be de-emphasized due to their easy replacement provided by competing offerings.

TST Challenge

Analyze and report in the following diagram the critical dimensions of the EP relating to the following business: Netflix streaming platform.* Pay attention to the main EBBs, qualify them through

---

*Netflix is a world-leading entertainment streaming platform recognized for its extensive library of movies, TV series, documentaries, and original content. Pioneering the way we consume visual media, Netflix offers a seamless and diverse viewing experience to subscribers worldwide. As a leader in the digital entertainment industry, Netflix has become the go-to destination for a rich and seamless entertainment experience. (www.netflix.com)

EQs and report the corresponding EBKs. Use the templates provided as follows (Figure 2.4).

EXPERIENTIAL PERFORMANCE		
EXPERIENTIAL BUILDING BLOCKS (EBB)	EXPERIENTIAL QUALITY (EQ)	EXPERIENTIAL BENCHMARK (EBK)
What are the relevant aspects of the customer experience?	In which way do these aspects create more value?	Compared to what substitute/similar experiences?
With Netflix the user can	How?	Differently from ....

Figure 2.4 Experiential performance worksheet

TST Practice #2 Transforming the Business Model Logic by Stretching the Experiential Performance

The second BML transformational practice is *stretching*, which can be defined as the process of emphasizing or de-emphasizing certain aspects of the *EP* related to a specific offering, that is, a product, a service, a platform, or whatever is at the core of a business model. After having identified and qualified the different EBBs, EQs, and EBKs of the *EP* (Step 1 to Step 3 in the previous section), you can start thinking about which of the aspects of the EP you will emphasize or de-emphasize by acting upon one or more EP's subdimensions. This means that the EP can be stretched in the following three ways:

Stretching by Introducing or Removing Experiential Building Blocks

First, you can stretch your EP by removing and adding one or more new EBBs to the current customer experience. For instance, assume you are the manager of Eat&Go, a fast food restaurant. Over the years, you've seen young couples, families, professionals, and teens lining up at the counters, eagerly waiting for their meals. They'd grab the first available table and enjoy their food while multitasking—making calls, working on projects, or even playing with their fries. For 10 years, it has been clear the type of experience your customers want: eat tasty food, eat it cheaply, and eat it fast. Now, picture yourself 10 years later, watching your restaurant's once-bustling tables grow increasingly vacant, while a new organic food bar across the street draws a constant crowd. In contrast to the vibrant green walls of the organic establishment, your space looks outdated, with weathered yellow plastic chairs and wornout iron counters. What's more, your renowned $1.50 chocolate milkshake seems to have been replaced by the $4 green juice, adored by the neighborhood's stylish schoolgirls. Additionally, you've noticed that customers at the organic place are happy to wait 20 minutes for a homemade quinoa salad, unlike your customers who used to expect their XL burger in under three minutes. You realize that customer preferences have changed, and to stay viable, you need to adapt your current EP. Put simply, it's time for a transformation—a *stretching* of your current EP toward a new paradigm. So, you start thinking about what you could change to evolve your customer experience.

One way to start can be removing one or more of your current EBBs and adding new ones. Suppose that your current EBBs are summarized as follows:

- EBB1. With Eat&Go, the customer can get a fast and quick meal.
- EBB2. With Eat&Go, the customer can eat a full meal while doing other activities.
- EBB3. With Eat&Go, customers can choose the meal that best suits their demands.

Suppose you want to turn Eat&Go into a fast-food restaurant in tune with customers who care about healthy food preparation and the quality of the ingredients (eventually organic products). To accomplish this, you can stretch many of the possibilities offered in your current business logic into something different.

Take EBB1: With Eat&Go, the customer can get a fast and quick meal. This can be replaced with a new EBB: With Eat&Go, the customer can cook a fast and quick meal.

In this way, the customer can keep the food preparation and use of certain potentially unhealthy ingredients, such as fat or excessive salt, under their control. Consequently, the new possibility of cooking the food provides a different experience while preserving the experience factors, such as the speed of the meal.

An alternative way of providing an experience in tune with strict customer control of meal preparation could be stretching EBB2: *With Eat&Go, the customer can eat a full meal while doing other activities*, by introducing the possibility of watching the food being prepared in a kitchen show. Thus, it can be replaced by a new EBB: *With Eat&Go, the customer can attend the preparation of a full meal while doing other activities*.

What about the customers' sensitivity to quality ingredients? To address this concern, you can remove EBB3: *With Eat&Go, customers can choose the meal that best suits their needs*. Secondly, you can introduce a new option for selecting ingredients through a new EBB: *With Eat&Go, customers can obtain information and select the ingredients for the meal that best suits their preferences (Figure 2.5)*.

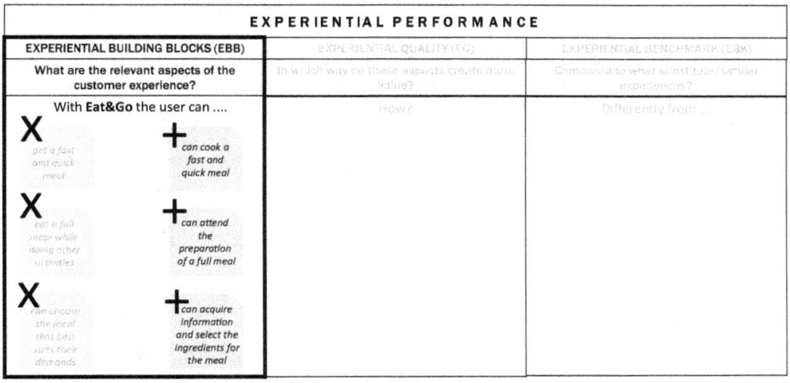

Figure 2.5 Stretching by introducing and removing EBBs

Stretching by Altering the Experiential Quality

As a second approach to *stretch* and redesign the EP, you could leverage the EQ, altering specific quality attributes within one or more existing EBBs. Imagine this scenario: you're a rising t-shirt designer who just launched your first brand, Ts4all, with a unique mission—to help everyone find their perfect t-shirt. Over the years, you've heard friends and colleagues complain about the difficulty of finding the right t-shirt for different occasions—whether it's a V-neck to pair with a formal suit or an oversized one for a trendy gym look. Traditional stores usually offer just one style in different sizes. Your idea was to improve this by creating a store with t-shirts in every possible fit, color, material, and size. You defined your EP as: *With Ts4all, the customer can find fashionable t-shirts "in a more accessible way,"* compared to other apparel retailers. However, a few months post launch, you notice that sales could be better, and your customers seem more bewildered than delighted by the vast array of choices. You observe their perplexed expressions in front of piles of white t-shirts bearing different labels, and it dawns on you that they require guidance during their shopping process. You still want your customers to find their perfect t-shirt, but their experience must evolve.

Suppose you shift the EQ from: *With Ts4all, the customer can find fashionable t-shirts "in a more accessible way"* to: *With Ts4all, the customer can find fashionable t-shirts "in a more custom way."* By altering the EQ, you'll need to contemplate a transformation of your current EP that enables customers not only to search and find but also to be assisted in locating the perfect t-shirt tailored to their specific needs. To achieve this, you could replace the extensive product inventory with a personalized service, where customers can complete a form specifying their preferences for color, size, fit, material, and occasion. A shopping assistant will then locate the ideal t-shirt for them. Some aspects of the physical space, such as the extensive area dedicated to displaying t-shirt piles, would be de-emphasized. This would create space for an extended counter where customers can await their customized t-shirts. Other aspects of the EP, such as customer service and staff training,

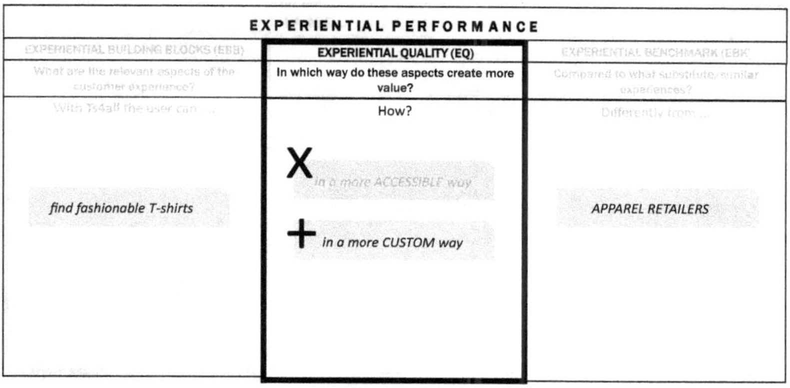

EXPERIENTIAL PERFORMANCE		
EXPERIENTIAL BUILDING BLOCKS (EBB)	EXPERIENTIAL QUALITY (EQ)	EXPERIENTIAL BENCHMARK (EBK)
What are the relevant aspects of the customer experience?	In which way do these aspects create more value?	Compared to what substitute/similar experiences?
With Ts4all the user can ...	How?	Differently from ...
find fashionable T-shirts	**X** in a more ACCESSIBLE way **+** in a more CUSTOM way	APPAREL RETAILERS

Figure 2.6 Stretching by altering the EQ

would become more pivotal. Consequently, altering one EBB's EQ will lead to a comprehensive transformation of the entire EP (Figure 2.6).

Stretching by Shifting the Experiential Benchmark

As a third approach to stratching, you could shift the EBK of your EBBs from one business domain to another, while keeping the EQ consistent. Let's consider the scenario where you run a wristwatch business, FunWatch. Your product line is characterized by contemporary design and high-quality materials. These watches are typically retailed in fashion concept stores or jewelry boutiques, with the aim of persuading potential customers to choose the elegant timepiece as a unique birthday gift over a conventional golden bracelet or a costly purse. While watches do offer functionality—an advantage over jewelry —their main appeal is their style. In the fashion accessories market, where watches have the functional edge of timekeeping compared to jewelry you define your EBK as follows: *With FunWatch, the customer can buy a luxury item in a more functional way than buying jewels.*

However, as similar offerings to FunWatch begin appearing on jewelry boutique shelves, often at more competitive prices, you see that focusing your Experiential Performance (EP) on the jewelry EBK is becoming less profitable. Consequently, you opt to return to the conventional watch business realm. You launch a flagship store where

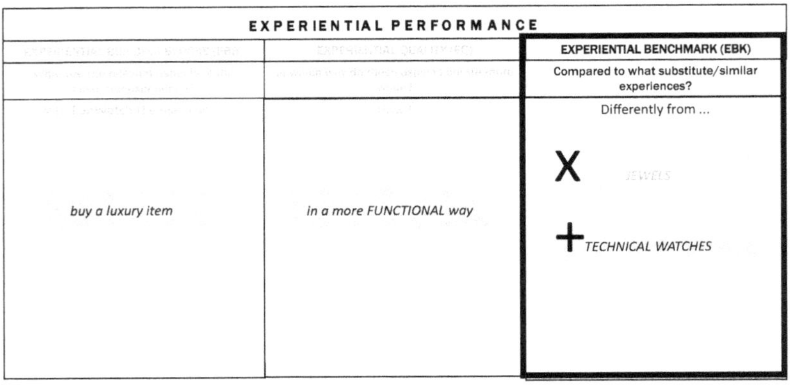

EXPERIENTIAL PERFORMANCE		
		EXPERIENTIAL BENCHMARK (EBK)
		Compared to what substitute/similar experiences?
		Differently from ...
buy a luxury item	in a more FUNCTIONAL way	X JEWELS
		+ TECHNICAL WATCHES

Figure 2.7 Stretching by shifting the EBK

customers are fully immersed in the FunWatch experience, perceiving the product's value as both a fashion accessory and a functional timepiece. Consequently, you'll accentuate both facets of product differentiation—the stylish design and premium materials, as well as factors related to the watch's performance, such as the watch glass, water resistance, and the watch movement.

While you may retain certain attributes characteristic of a jewelry shop, such as meticulous customer service and fancy interiors, you'll complement them with a highly trained staff capable of providing technical information about the watches' functionality. Your new EP is then defined as: *With FunWatch, the customer can buy a luxury item in a more functional way than technical watches.* In the first case, FunWatch's experiential benchmark is defined in the context of jewelry boutiques. In the second case, the functional aspect of the experience is expanded because it is defined within the context of watch stores (Figure 2.7).

Key Takeaways

In summary, to transform the BML through stretching, you can manipulate the EP of a specific offering by leveraging its three subdimensions. This can be achieved by:

1. Introducing or removing one or more new EBBs to the existing EP.
2. Altering the EQ aspects of one or more current EBBs.
3. Shifting the EBK of one or more EBBs from one business context to another while maintaining the same EQ.

By executing one of these operations, you'll notice that certain facets of the EP become more or less pertinent to the new user experience. This, in turn, catalyzes a transformation of the entire BML underlying your value offering.

Business Case Example

Stretching the Performance of Starbucks Coffee Shop: The Reserve Roastery

When Starbucks made the strategic decision to enter the high-end coffee market in 2010, they introduced the Starbucks Reserve program, offering small-batch Arabica coffee for sale online and in select retail locations. Encouraged by the success of this premium product line, the company embarked on a new venture by launching the first Starbucks Reserve locations, promising a completely novel experience for their customers. The inaugural Starbucks Reserve Roastery debuted in Seattle in 2014, followed by openings in Washington DC (2014), Shanghai (2017), Milan (2018), New York City (2018), Tokyo (2019), and Chicago (2019). In stark contrast to standard Starbucks locations, Roastery stores span thousands of square feet and are designed to provide an immersive experience. Often compared to a theme park, these stores allow customers to participate in coffee tastings, enjoy coffee-inspired cocktails in a dedicated lounge, and explore culinary offerings that reflect the local traditions of each city. For example, the Milan Roastery collaborates with the renowned Milanese bakery 'Princi' to offer authentic Italian aperitivo experiences. Additionally, staff receive specialized training to educate customers about the origins and details of their orders. This Roastery concept marks a notable departure from Starbucks' original BML. Indeed, through a strategic shift in various facets of the BML's EP—encompassing the environment, coffee quality, food selection, service standards, and staff training—customers are treated to an entirely fresh experience that redefines the conventional Starbucks coffee shop. Some EBBs unique to the classic Starbucks EP have been incorporated, while others have been replaced. For example, EBB 1: "The opportunity for the customer to spend time in diverse ways while enjoying a great cup of coffee" has evolved into EBBnew: "The opportunity for the customer to spend time in an exclusive location while savoring a great cup of coffee." This transformation has redefined the concept of Starbucks as a *third place*. What was once a casual stop in daily routines has now become a destination similar to a museum visit, attracting visitors who intentionally seek a unique way to spend their leisure time. This stretching transformation is also evident in the enhancement of quality (EQ) in specific aspects of the traditional Starbucks EP. For instance, the shift from "The possibility for the customer to enjoy a drink in a more comfortable location" to "The possibility for the customer to enjoy a drink in a more exclusive location" marks a notable upgrade. While plush velvet armchairs, plenty of power outlets, and free Wi-Fi were key draws in the traditional Starbucks EP, the Roastery focuses on features like the impressive roasting equipment, cozy lounge areas, and a curated selection of gourmet offerings as its main attractions. Ultimately, the transformative impact of stretching is most pronounced in the shift of the EBK. Whereas the conventional Starbucks EP was defined in relation to other coffee shops, the Roastery surpasses the confines of a standard local coffee bar experience, positioning itself to rival businesses in entirely distinct domains, including museums, fancy restaurants, and chic bars. This shift underscores the Roastery's ambition to offer a truly unique and elevated EP.

Chapter Overview

In this chapter, we have illustrated the second element of the BML: the *Experiential Performance (EP)*. This defines the aspects of the customer experience that hold significance in the value-creation process and how these elements are prioritized. The EP can be analyzed and designed by a three-step process in which you define the Experiential Building Block (EBB), the Experiential Benchmark (EBK), and, finally, the Experiential Quality (EQ). Furthermore, we have introduced the second transformative practice within the BML framework: the *stretching*. This practice involves the strategic emphasis or de-emphasis of specific aspects within the EP of a particular offering, utilizing its subdimensions to bring about a targeted transformation.

CHAPTER 3

Sharing the Resources

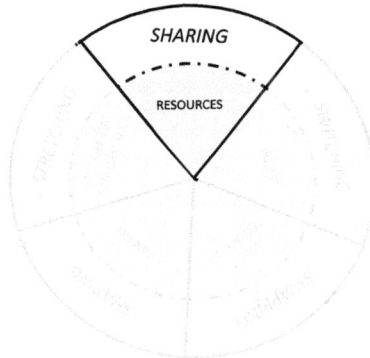

Figure 3.1 Sharing the resources

What Will You Learn?

You will:

- Understand, in a Business Model Logic (BML), which aspects define the resources.
- Learn how to analyze the resources in a BML.
- Learn how to design the resources regime in your BML practically.
- Understand how to trigger a BML transformation by sharing the resources.
- Understand the implications of sharing the resources in a BML from real-world business examples (Figure 3.1).

Element #3 the Resources: Learning How to Win

A firm is essentially a pool of resources the utilization of which is organized in an administrative framework.

—Edith Penrose, 1959

From a business standpoint, a resource encompasses anything, or anyone, that a company requires to carry out its operations effectively, achieve excellence, and thrive. This perspective gained prominence in the early 1990s with the emergence of strategic management theories, particularly the resource-based view (RBV), which posited that a company's performance is primarily shaped by the resources it possesses rather than the industry's overall profitability (as suggested by The Positioning School). These resources can take various forms:

- Physical assets: Tangible resources such as manufacturing facilities, vehicles, and plants.
- Intellectual assets: Intangible but valuable assets such as brands, partnerships, proprietary knowledge, and customer databases.
- Human capital: The expertise and skills of employees, often exemplified by skilled sales personnel or engineers.
- Financial resources: Monetary assets, covering cash reserves, lines of credit, and stock option pools, among others.

Each of these resource categories may play a crucial role in a company's ability to function effectively and thrive in the business environment. For instance, large retailers such as Amazon and Walmart place a substantial emphasis on physical resources, relying on extensive logistics facilities and distribution networks to maintain competitiveness in their respective markets. Conversely, companies such as Nike and Microsoft have predominantly harnessed intellectual resources, leveraging their brand equity and software development expertise to solidify their market share. In certain industries, human resources serve as the cornerstone of competitive advantage. This is notably observed in knowledge-intensive sectors like biopharma, where companies heavily depend on skilled scientists for groundbreaking drug discoveries and dynamic sales teams for effective integration into the health care delivery system. Meanwhile, certain business models pivot significantly on financial resources for value creation. Take, for example, Ericsson, the Swedish telecommunications company, which historically leveraged capital market borrowings to extend vendor financing, strategically securing customers over its competitors.

To succeed strategically, a company must understand the market environment—figuring out "where to play." However, advocates of the Resource-Based View (RBV) argue that knowing the market rules isn't enough. They believe that understanding a company's key resources and assets offers better insight into "how to win" against competitors. Take Disney, for example. It started as an animation company and has grown into a leading entertainment and media giant with film, TV, and theme parks. When Netflix nearly monopolized the home entertainment industry through its continuously improving algorithmic suggestion system and significant investments in fresh content, Disney recognized that competition in the industry revolved around two crucial resources: compelling content and robust streaming platforms.

With an extensive portfolio of iconic characters—from Mickey and Minnie Mouse to the Disney princesses—as well as strategic acquisitions of Marvel Studios, Pixar, Lucasfilm, and 20th Century Fox, Disney possesses an ever-expanding catalog of movies and shows, appealing to both adults and children. This arsenal enabled them to compete head-to-head with streaming leaders. On the other hand, Netflix capitalized on a highly efficient platform and years of experience in data acquisition to anticipate users' preferences. Rather than embarking on the development of an entirely new platform to rival Netflix, Disney opted to acquire an existing streaming service—Hulu—thereby leveraging its primary key asset: an extensive library of entertainment content. Consequently, in 2019, the "mouse struck back" with the launch of Disney Plus, its official streaming service. With over 100 million subscribers in just 16 months, it is expected to outperform competitors such as Amazon and Netflix in the coming years. By understanding "where to play"—through a keen awareness of entertainment market trends—and "how to win"—via a clear assessment of its key assets—Disney demonstrated its ability to redefine its BML and compete in the streaming wars.

While a firm's available resources ultimately drive its performance, not all resources hold equal importance or potential for constituting a sustainable competitive advantage. For instance, in the case of an e-commerce company, resources such as cash and trucks are not considered strategic, as competitors can readily acquire them. Instead, companies like Amazon prefer to leverage their globally renowned brand to introduce their own branded products, thereby gaining an edge over competing platforms, and even indirect rivals. A prime example is the success of *Alexa*, Amazon's *know-it-all* digital assistant, which successfully competed with Google Home by integrating online shopping with real-time updates on Amazon deliveries and offering Amazon Prime users unlimited access to the Amazon Music catalog. Identifying and prioritizing the key resources that are both relevant and strategic is essential in creating value within your BML. It's worth noting that a resource need not be something a firm owns outright, but also something it has temporary *access to*. The rise of sharing economy companies serves as a compelling example of how some of the most strategic and value-creating resources are no longer exclusively owned by the company, but are held collectively by its user community. Airbnb, for instance, has emerged as a popular lodging option, capturing a significant market share from major hotel industry players, all by leveraging the strategic resources of its users—hosts' apartments and rooms. The same principle applies to companies such as Uber with cars and Neighbor with storage units. These companies have demonstrated that ownership and control over the most strategic resources aren't always prerequisites for success. On the contrary, sharing resources with external stakeholders, including partners and users, can enhance the perceived value for end customers, leading to benefits such as lower prices or greater service availability. Therefore, when designing a BML after identifying key resources, it's crucial to formulate hypotheses about which stakeholders will be involved based on the key resources they have access to.

Wrap-Up Questions

To sum up, the resources in the BML can be defined by two basic questions:

1. What are the key resources of the value creation process? and
2. What are the actors that control these resources?

Warm-Up Task

1. Pick a successful product or service that you know well. Name at least three key resources you think are unique for the company.

Brand/Product:_____

1._____
2._____
3._____
4._____
5._____

2. Think about the resources that you mentioned. Who do you think is in control of them?

1._____
2._____
3._____
4._____
5._____

Understanding the Resources

As highlighted in the initial section, defining the third element of the BML—*resources*—is dependent on two critical factors. First, identify the strategic resources that lend distinctiveness to the firm's value offering, and then determine how the organization receives direct or indirect access to them. To assess and design the resources within your business model, use a simple analytic framework consisting of two basic steps

- **Step 1. Identify the Key Resources**: This step aims to define the relevant resources within your BML.
- **Step 2. Identify the Resource Regime**: This step involves determining who holds control over the key resources, whether its partners, customers, or the company itself.

The combination of key resources and the identification of the resource regime collectively delineate the *resources* that underpin the BML (Figure 3.2).

Step 1. Identify the Key Resources

Key resources are essential assets that make a company's value offering stand out and help it outperform competitors. To identify unique resources, look at the definition of Experiential Performance (EP) from Chapter 2. This involves examining the Experiential Building Blocks (EBBs), their Experiential Quality (EQ), and the Experiential Benchmark (EBK) to find the resources contributing to the unique EP..

In more specific terms, identifying a key resource involves answering questions such as:

- Does the resource play a crucial role in providing the user with the specific EBB that characterizes the business logic?

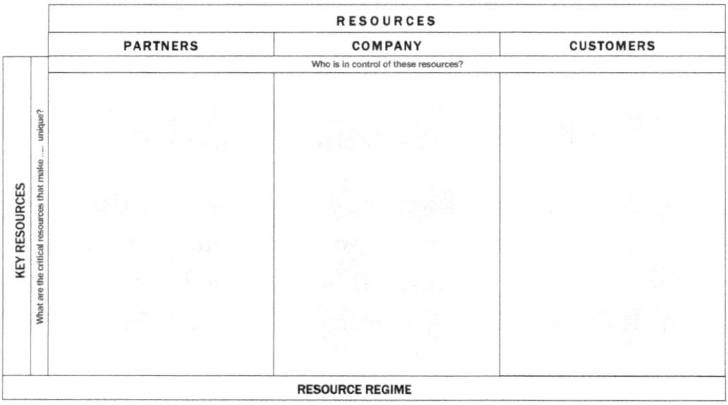

Figure 3.2 Resources subdimensions

- Is the resource essential for the EQ of the EBB?
- Can the resource contribute to multiple experiences within the business logic?

As a general guideline, if a particular resource enhances the quality of more than one EBB, it can be deemed a key resource.

Using *Compasses Magazine* as an example, an architecture and design magazine with a particular focus on the Middle East, let's examine its EP through the following scenario: *With Compasses, users gain access to valuable insights about architecture and design* (EBB1) in a way that is both *more accessible* (EQ1) and *more environmentally sustainable* (EQ2), particularly when compared to *magazines that exclusively produce print editions* (EBQ1).

In this context, the *digital platform* emerges as a key resource. It enables readers to access the magazine online at their convenience through various devices (EQ1: providing a more accessible experience) while also contributing to sustainability efforts by reducing paper consumption (EQ2: promoting environmental sustainability).

Step 2. Identify the Resource Regime

The resource regime refers to the ownership and control of a company's key resources. However, as mentioned, not all resources need to be owned by the company. Instead, the company can use resources from external sources, such as partners who manage outsourced activities or customers who provide essential resources for creating value. Therefore, the final step in defining resources within the BML is determining the category of actors—whether they are companies, partners, or customers—that exert full control over key resources.

Taking the example of *Compasses Magazine*, let's identify *articles* and *pictures* as key resources for EBB1: *With Compasses, the user can have the possibility of gaining knowledge about architecture and design.* The articles are typically written and edited by professionals employed directly by the company. On the other hand, the pictures are sourced through licensing agreements with various professional freelance photographers,

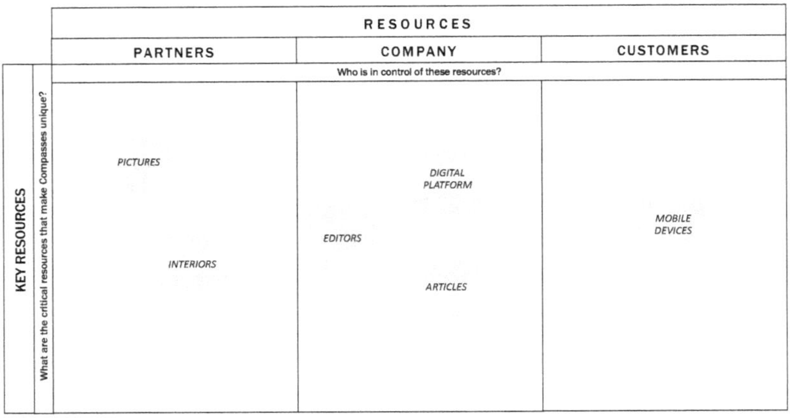

Figure 3.3 Compasses magazine resources

providing diverse perspectives with each publication. Consequently, while the company owns the key resource article, the second key resource *pictures* is owned by a partner, specifically freelance photographers (Figure 3.3).

So What?

In essence, resources within a BML are characterized by two primary dimensions: key resources and resource regime. Through the definition of these elements, we gain profound insights, allowing us to reconsider the distribution of our assets. This may involve experimenting with processes of sharing or taking back control of strategic resources, which can potentially trigger a transformative shift in the entire BML (Figure 3.4).

TST Challenge

Analyze and report in the following diagram the key two dimensions of the resources of the following business: BlaBlaCar[*]. Identify the key resources and their respective resource regime, placing them within the corresponding box indicating the actor in control. Utilize the provided templates.

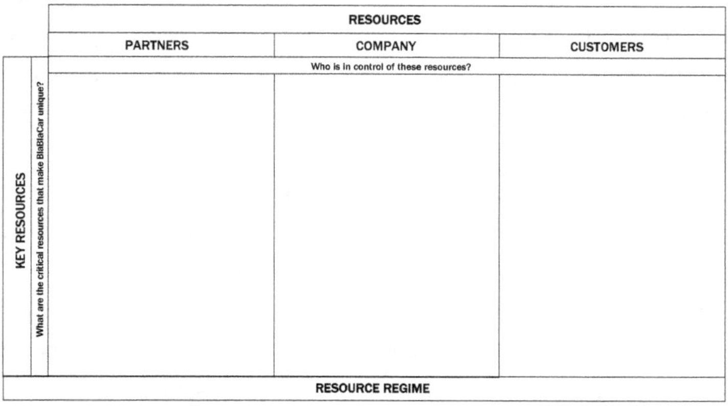

Figure 3.4 Resources worksheet

TST Practice #3 Transforming the Business Model Logic by Sharing the Resources

The third BML transformation is *sharing*. This practice involves redefining the resource regime of *resources*, which essentially entails transferring ownership of pertinent resources from the company to partners and/or customers, and vice versa. Through this process, it becomes possible to introduce innovation and fundamentally reshape the existing BML. Once you have identified the key resources and their respective resource regime within your product or service's BML (as outlined in Steps 1 and 2 in the

---

[*]BlaBlaCar is a prominent global platform that revolutionizes long-distance travel by connecting drivers with available seats to passengers headed in the same direction. BlaBlaCar has become a trusted community for cost-effective and eco-friendly journeys. The platform offers a convenient and efficient way for individuals to share rides, reducing transportation costs and environmental impact www.blablacar.co.uk.

preceding section), it's time to consider how the original resource regime can be reimagined by altering the actors that control them. This means that resources can be reconfigured in two distinct ways:

Insharing the Resources

The first approach consists in *insharing* the resources, which involves taking control over resources or assets that were previously controlled by a third party. This practice leverages key resources for value creation, assuming that these insourced resources were previously owned and fully controlled by the company's partners or customers. This practice leverages key resources for value creation, assuming that these insourced resources were previously owned and fully controlled by the company's partners or customers. With a market cap of $1.3 trillion, Amazon has not gotten where it is today by resting on its laurels. The size and variety of Amazon's service portfolio show that the company values innovation and has the ability to enter (and disrupt) new industries.

Amazon's extensive and diverse service portfolio showcases a commitment to innovation and a capacity to enter and disrupt new industries. Since 2014, the e-commerce giant has invested millions of dollars in establishing its own logistics network, comprising a fleet of 70 cargo planes, 400,000 drivers globally, 40,000 semitrucks, and 30,000 delivery vans. This transition has shifted Amazon's shipping operations from almost entirely outsourced in 2013 (primarily to UPS and FedEx) to in-house management of two-thirds of its shipments. Additionally, Amazon's fleet now serves non-Amazon clients, enabling the company to compete directly with major parcel shipment firms such as USPS, UPS, and FedEx. By insourcing physical resources (planes, trucks, vans, etc.) that were previously controlled by external partners (e.g., FedEx, UPS), Amazon has not only reduced its reliance on third-party freighter services but has also established a new business sector, Amazon Logistics. This move substantially enhances the speed and efficiency of deliveries for its customers.

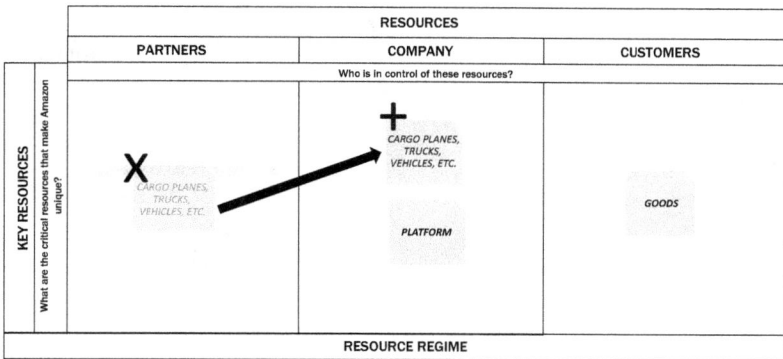

Figure 3.5 Insharing the resources

Through this sharing practice, Amazon aspires to fulfill the demand for "same-day delivery," contributing to a transformation in the e-commerce BML. This shift toward a more immediate shopping experience aligns with the immediacy typical of brick-and-mortar stores (Figure 3.5).

Outsharing the Resources

Another avenue for experimenting with BML transformation by altering the resource regime is *outsharing*. Outsharing involves the practice of transferring ownership or control of resources from the company to external partners or customers.

This practice entails leveraging resources that are no longer under the direct ownership of the company, but are instead held by external partners or even shared with customers. This can lead to the addition of new key resources in the resource regime. The underlying assumption is that the resources that are *outshared* were previously owned and fully controlled by the company. Consider how crowdfunding digital platforms have revolutionized the traditional approach to venture funding. In the conventional private investment model, the most critical resource, namely *capital*, is managed by the company's shareholders. They decide, based on their financial and management expertise, which companies or start-ups receive the necessary funding to grow their business. Crowdfunding digital platforms, particularly those following

		RESOURCES		
		PARTNERS	COMPANY	CUSTOMERS
KEY RESOURCES	What are the critical resources that make GoFundMe unique?		Who is in control of these resources? X *CAPITAL* ⟶ + *CAPITAL* *PLATFORM*	
			RESOURCE REGIME	

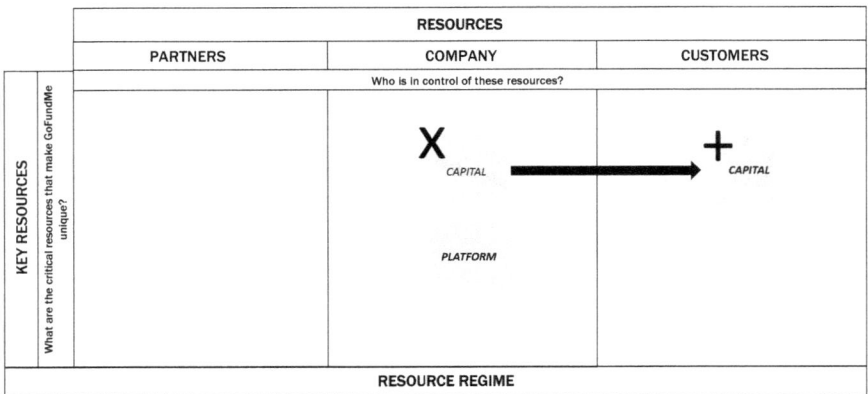

Figure 3.6 Outsharing the resources

a reward-based model such as Kickstarter, Indiegogo, and GoFundMe, have not only made funding more accessible but have also reshaped the traditional private investment BML. They identify new key resources and alter the resource control regime through a sharing process. As a result of this sharing process, the platform itself becomes a new key resource controlled by the company. While the company's most pivotal resource is the *platform* through which innovators can showcase their ideas and secure funding, the financial resources are now owned by the customers. In exchange for their funding, they receive a reward in the form of a product stemming from the idea that will be brought to market thanks to crowdfunding (Figure 3.6).

Key Takeaways

In summary, to transform the BML through sharing, you can modify the resource regime—altering the actors who control key resources. This can be achieved in two ways:

1. Outsharing: The company cedes control of resources that were previously owned and fully controlled by the company to external partners or customers.
2. Insharing: The company gains control of key resources that were previously owned and fully controlled by its external partners or customers.

By implementing one of these strategies, you can adjust the original portfolio and regime of key resources. This, in turn, can catalyze a transformation of the entire BML of your value offering.

Business Case Example

TaskRabbit: Leveraging Local Resources Through Neighborly Assistance

TaskRabbit Inc., established in 2008, stands as one of the early pioneers and notable success stories in the sharing economy. This multinational software application operates as a multisided online platform, enabling users to delegate errands or minor tasks to local contractors under the ethos of "neighbors helping neighbors." The platform acts as a peer-to-peer marketplace, connecting "TaskPosters" (individuals in need of specific services such as cleaning, product delivery, minor household repairs, and furniture assembly) with qualified TaskDoers (preapproved individuals available for these tasks at reasonable rates). Those seeking assistance can post their requests through the app, after which the company promptly links them with the nearest available TaskDoer, who then has the option to accept or decline the job within 30 minutes. Once the task is completed, payment and feedback can be submitted through the app. In this model, the most critical resource for value creation—the task itself—is not controlled by the company. Instead, it is outsourced to freelance worker who enjoys the flexibility of choosing their work hours and earning supplementary income at their convenience.

Simultaneously, TaskDoers benefit from a swift, cost-effective service facilitated by a vast network of workers with diverse skills and geographic coverage provided by the platform.

TaskRabbit exemplifies how, through outsharing essential resources such as tools and labor with a specific category of platform users (TaskDoers), it has innovatively and efficiently transformed the conventional small contractor business model.

Chapter Overview

This chapter discusses the third component of the BML: *resources*. This encompasses identifying key resources for value creation and identifying the actors with control over them. Analyzing and designing resources involves a two-step approach: first, recognizing the key resources and then establishing the corresponding resource regime. Subsequently, we delved into the third transformative practice within BML: *sharing*. Sharing entails reconfiguring the resource regime in the BML, achieved through *outsharing* or *insharing* of one or more key resources.

CHAPTER 4

Switching the Roles

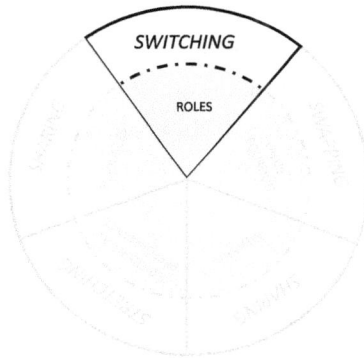

Figure 4.1 Switching the roles

What Will You Learn?

You will:

- Understand, in a Business Model Logic (BML), which aspects define the roles.
- Learn how to analyze the roles in a BML.
- Learn how to design the roles regime in your BML practically.
- Understand how to trigger a BML transformation by switching the roles.
- Understand the implications of switching the roles in a BML from real-world business examples.

Element #4 the Roles: A Matter of Responsibilities

Strategy is a commodity, execution is an art.

—Peter Drucker

In crafting a business model, it is important to delineate the *roles*, specifically pinpointing who holds responsibility for the key activities in the company's value creation process. Ever since Michael Porter introduced the concept of the firm's value chain in 1985, scholars and practitioners in management have come to perceive a company as a mix of distinct yet crucial activities. These are not merely seen as costs, but as steps toward increasing the value of the final product or service.

From the acquisition of raw materials and resources from suppliers (inbound logistics) to the provision of technical support postpurchase (after-sales services), every facet of operations can potentially influence a company's competitive advantage. While all activities contributing to the final product or service are vital, not all carry the same weight in delivering value or in setting our product or service apart. Business model analysis tools like the Business Model Canvas have guided us to focus on key activities—those processes, tasks, and efforts that are hard to replicate and that customers link to your product or service. These key activities encompass production, problem-solving, and platform management, all based on the company's overall business model, which includes its market, customer segments, and value proposition. From our perspective, a key activity is one that plays a crucial role in shaping the unique experience linked to a particular product or service. For instance, in examining Amazon's shopping experience, a standout activity that distinguishes it from conventional retailers like Walmart is the ability to evaluate products before purchase, thanks to user reviews. In a physical store, a wide array of cosmetic products can overwhelm someone looking for a simple hand moisturizer due to the numerous options and attractive packaging. On the other hand, when buying a hand moisturizer on Amazon, the star rating system immediately highlights which products to avoid—after all, who would choose a one-star item? Additionally, customer reviews provide accurate and detailed guidance on the best options. Thus, gathering and displaying feedback data becomes a key activity in Amazon's business model, setting its experience apart from competitors. Considering this, it is critical to first identify (and prioritize) in a business model the main activities that are strategically important in the creation of value.

Some of these activities may fall under the responsibility of the company's customers or external partners.

The self-service revolution in the retail industry provides numerous instances of how pivotal activities for value creation are delegated to customers rather than being directly managed by the company. Consider the transformative approach of IKEA in the furniture retailing business. At some point, we've all wielded an Ikea Allen key—whether wrestling with the instructions for a Malm drawer or debating with a partner over the ideal arrangement of Kallax shelves. The point is that we've all felt like "partial employees" of IKEA, tasked with picking, transporting, and assembling furniture pieces after a pilgrimage to the Blue Mecca. In this manner, IKEA has placed the customer at the heart of the product realization process, assigning specific roles within the flow of activities in its value chain. After all, IKEA's slogan, "Live Unboring," presages the considerable effort the customer will invest, along with the opportunity to proudly proclaim, "I made this," imbued with a genuine sense of accomplishment for those who aren't inherently adept at furniture assembly. Naturally, the extent of customer involvement varies across different business models. In the case of IKEA, we observe an engaged (and self-reliant) customer shouldering multiple roles in the company's value creation activities (e.g., product selection, warehousing retrieval, cashier interaction, payment, transportation, and assembly). Conversely, in a traditional furniture retailing setting, customers are primarily responsible for product selection, with assembly and delivery handled by the company and its partners. Hence, while crafting a BML and after identifying the key activities, it is vital to formulate assumptions regarding the actors who wield significant influence in the value creation process.

Wrap-Up Questions

In summary, roles within the BML can be determined by addressing two fundamental questions:

1. What are the key activities in the value creation process?
2. Who are the actors responsible for these activities?

Warm-Up Task

Choose a successful product or service that you are familiar with. Identify at least three activities that you believe are crucial in creating a distinctive experience associated with the product or service.

Brand/Product:_____

1._____
2._____
3._____
4._____
5._____

Consider the activities you mentioned. Who do you believe is in control of them?

1._____
2._____
3._____
4._____
5._____

Understanding the Roles

As mentioned earlier, external actors such as partners or customers can play significant roles in a company's value creation process by engaging in key activities that contribute to creating a unique experience. Therefore, the identification of these key activities, understanding their flow, and recognizing the actors who perform them is crucial in analyzing the *roles* within a BML. To effectively analyze and design roles for a product or service, follow these three simple steps:

- Step 1. Identify the Flow of Key Activities: Gain insight into the activities that hold relevance in your BML.
- Step 2. Map the Flow of Key Activities: Understand the sequence in which key activities are integrated into your BML.
- Step 3. Identify the Key Roles: Define who is responsible for these key activities, whether they are partners, customers, or the company itself.

By combining the identification of key activities, understanding their flow, and pinpointing the responsible actors, you can establish the roles within the BML (Figure 4.2).

Step 1. Identify the Flow of Key Activities

Key activities specifically pertain to tasks and processes that contribute to the unique experience associated with the consumption or acquisition of a firm's value offering, ultimately aiming for superior market performance. Much like resources, a straightforward method to identify whether an activity is key is to refer to the definition of Experiential Performance (EP) (refer to Chapter 2). This involves examining

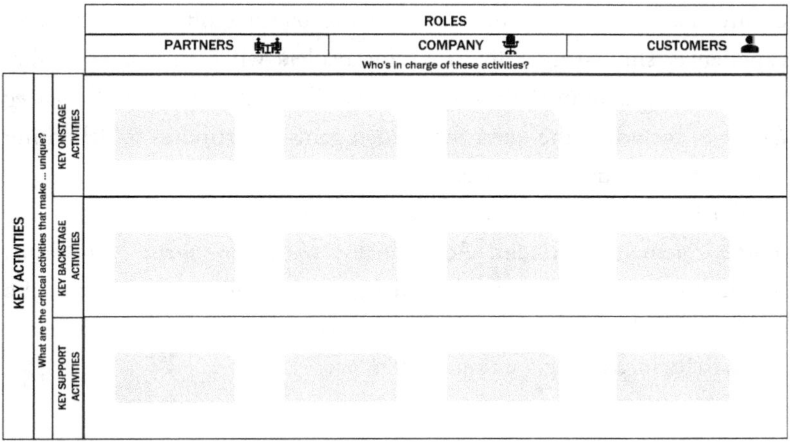

Figure 4.2 Roles subdimensions

the different Experiential Building Blocks (EBBs), the corresponding Experiential Quality (EQ), and considering the relative Experiential Benchmark (EBK). By doing so, it becomes possible to pinpoint which activities contribute to the distinctiveness of the EP. To facilitate this, one can identify key activities by answering questions such as:

- Is the activity necessary for providing the user with the specific EBB that characterizes the BML?
- Does the activity significantly influence the EQ of a specific EBB?
- Can the activity contribute to multiple EBBs within the business logic?

Let's revisit the example of *Compasses Magazine*, an architecture and design magazine with a geographical focus on the Middle East, to illustrate its EP:

- EP1: *With Compasses, the user can take virtual architectural tours around the world* (EBB1) *in a more accessible way* (EQ1) *compared to travel tours* (EBK1).
- EP2: *With Compasses, the user can find inspiration for future home decoration* (EBB2) *in a more original way* (EQ2) *compared to magazines without a specific geographical focus* (EBK2).

In the case of EP1, a key activity may involve *taking photographs* to ensure that the quality and angles of the pictures offer an immersive experience, simulating a live tour for readers while they comfortably read the magazine in their armchairs. Similarly, the *selection of shooting locations*, including the quest for hidden gems, contributes to delighting readers with a sense of discovery.

For EP2, the key activities of *taking photographs* and *selecting shooting locations* remain pertinent. Additionally, *the arrangement of interiors*, which involves the placement of design pieces in a way that specific details catch the reader's attention and inspire them, can be considered a key activity in creating a unique experience

---

Design Tips

Define key activities by simply answering to the question: "Does the activity x allow the EBBX to more EQx?" or "Does the activity x allow the EBBX to more EQy?" or "Does the activity x allow the EBBY to more EQx?" As a general rule, if the answer is "yes" for at least two of these questions, you can consider it as a key resource.

Step 2. Map the Flow of Key Activities

Once we have identified the key activities that contribute to creating a unique experience associated with a specific product or service, we can proceed to define the flow of activities—that is, the sequence in which these activities are performed. From this perspective, we can categorize the key activities into three types:

- **Key Onstage Activities (KOA):** These are the activities visible to the customer during the delivery of the service or product, directly adding value (e.g., a waiter serving at a table).
- **Key Backstage Activities (KBA):** These activities occur behind the scenes and are not visible to the customer, yet they are essential for creating value (e.g., a chef cooking in the kitchen). They play a crucial role in supporting on-stage activities.
- **Key Support Activities (KSA):** These activities are indirectly involved in the value creation process, supporting the execution of backstage activities (e.g., a fisherman providing fresh fish to be cooked by the chef).

Let's revisit the example of *Compasses Magazine*. Suppose there's a digital version of the magazine with additional content available for free to users with an annual subscription. To initiate their experience with *Compasses Magazine*, users must download the app, which is essential for reading the magazine on their digital devices. Therefore, we can classify *Compasses App download* as a KOA. Once the app is downloaded, users can start immersing themselves in the magazine, exploring exotic locations, and drawing inspiration from interior design through high-quality photographic and video content that accompanies the articles. This immersive reading experience is made possible by the dedicated efforts of the magazine editors, who leverage their expertise to curate and present the most evocative content for an exceptional reading experience. In this case, the *management of digital content* becomes a KBA.

Additionally, we can envision that the editors' work is facilitated by hiring freelance photographers and digital content creators who travel to distant locations, tirelessly capturing the best shots and videos. Hence, *visual media production* emerges as a KSA in the value creation process.

Step 3. Identify the Key Roles

Once the sequence of activities is established, the next step is to identify the key actors involved in each of the onstage, backstage, and support activities. It's important to note that key activities can be carried out by the company, external partners, or even customers, all of whom can actively participate in the value creation process. Using the key activities we mapped in the previous section regarding Compasses World, we can already observe the distribution:

- KOA1. *Compasses App download*: This is the responsibility of the "Customer."
- KBA1. *Management of digital contents*: This falls under the responsibility of the "Company."
- KSA1. *Visual Media Production*: This is the responsibility of partners, namely freelance photographers and video-makers who collaborate with the company (Figure 4.3).

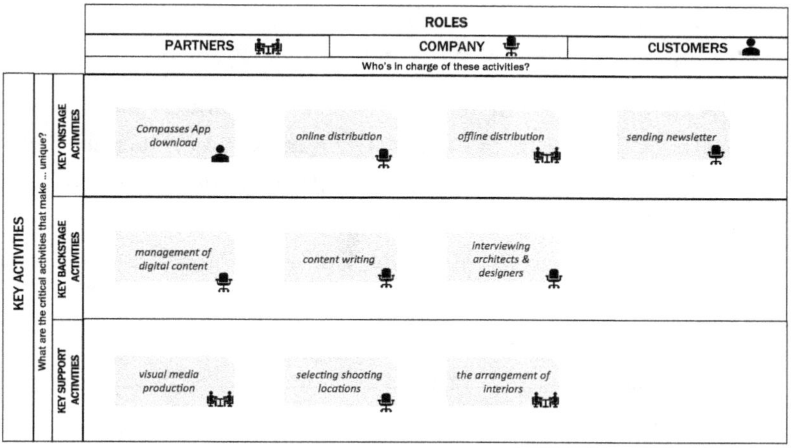

	ROLES		
PARTNERS 👥	COMPANY 💺		CUSTOMERS 👤
	Who's in charge of these activities?		

KEY ACTIVITIES — What are the critical activities that make ... unique?

KEY ONSTAGE ACTIVITIES

| Compasses App download 👤 | online distribution 💺 | offline distribution 👥 | sending newsletter 💺 |

KEY BACKSTAGE ACTIVITIES

| management of digital content 💺 | content writing 💺 | interviewing architects & designers 💺 | |

KEY SUPPORT ACTIVITIES

| visual media production 👥 | selecting shooting locations 💺 | the arrangement of interiors 👥 | |

Figure 4.3 Compasses roles

In summary, to define the *roles* in a BML, we first identify the key activities. Next, we map their flow by categorizing them into onstage, backstage, and support activities. Finally, we ascertain which actor—be it the company, partners, or customers—is accountable for each key activity (key roles).

So What?

By defining the key activities that provide a unique experience for users, understanding their flow, and identifying the key roles involved, we will gain profound insights. These insights will empower us to not only evolve the existing roles but also initiate a more efficient transformation of the entire BML. Through the identification of key activities, we can focus on tasks and processes that are pivotal for value creation. This enables us to channel our experimentation efforts toward areas with the highest potential for transformative impact on the entire BML. Moreover, understanding activity flows and the roles associated with them equips us with agile tools for exploring alternative transformational strategies, as we will discuss in the next section.

The TST Challenge

Analyze and report in the following diagram the critical dimensions of the roles relating to the following business: Lego. Identify and chart the key activities, placing them within the designated box to denote their respective level. Additionally, specify which category of actor is responsible for each activity. Utilize the provided templates (Figure 4.4).

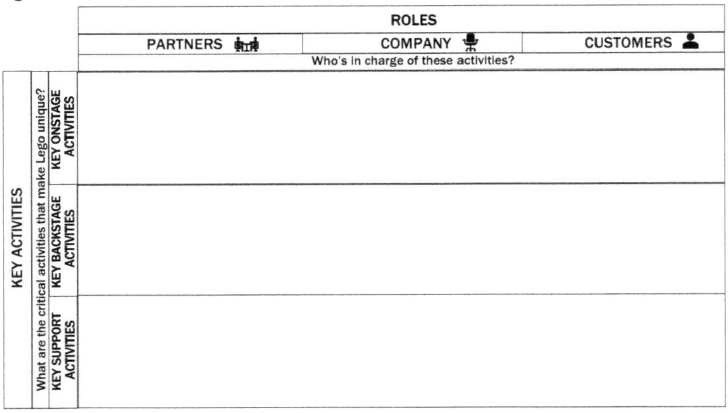

Figure 4.4 Roles worksheet

TST Practice #4 Transforming the Business Model Logic by Switching the Roles

To experiment with alternative BML transformations starting from the *roles* element, you can use the switching creative practice.

The switching practice refers to the process of changing the flow of key activities (KOA; KBA; KSA) and assigning new key roles for the conduct of relevant activities in the current BML. Put simply, by altering the sequence of tasks and processes crucial to the customer

*LEGO, a global powerhouse in the toy industry, is known for its iconic interlocking bricks that have sparked creativity and imagination in millions of children and adults alike. Offering a vast array of themed sets, from cityscapes to fantasy worlds, LEGO invites individuals of all ages to build, explore, and invent (https://lego.com).

journey, as well as redefining the responsible actors, it is possible to initiate a transformation that ripples through all other elements of the BML. Following the identification of key activities and roles (refer to Step 1 and Step 2 in the preceding section), you can implement *role* transformations in two distinct manners (Figure 4.5).

Switching by Changing the Flow of Activities

Changing the flow of activities means modifying the order—or the hierarchy—according to which relevant processes and tasks contribute to value creation.

There are a few options to change the flow of activities to ultimately transform the entire *roles* element. Here are a few examples of *switching by changing the flow of activities*.

From Backstage to Onstage activities (KBA >KOA)

Elevating backstage activities to onstage activities involves unveiling certain operations to the customer, which were previously concealed. Imagine a charming local restaurant known for its delicious regional dishes. Diners, intrigued by the wonderful meal, might want to learn more about how a particular dish is made. They could frequently ask the waitstaff about the techniques and ingredients behind what they're enjoying. To ease the staff's burden and clear up any uncertainty, someone suggests installing a transparent partition between the kitchen and dining area. This would allow customers to watch the cooking process, transforming it into an engaging culinary show where they can discover firsthand the "culinary secrets" they are eager to learn.

In this scenario, what once constituted a behind-the-scenes activity, KBA: *food preparation*, turns into an onstage activity, now observable to the customers as KOA: *food preparation*. This transformation provides customers with an entirely new and immersive dining experience.

From Onstage to Backstage (KOA >KBA)

Turning onstage into backstage activities implies that tasks once visible to the customer are now concealed from their experience. On-demand streaming platforms are a delight for avid binge-watchers, offering an extensive array of movies, TV series, and shows. However, the downside is that with so many options, picking something that matches your preferences and mood can feel like it takes longer than actually watching the movie or show. Algorithm-driven platforms like Netflix have made great progress in reducing this frustration. Through adept data collection and analysis of users' viewing history and preferences, they automatically recommend content, preempting what the viewer might enjoy.

In this scenario, the once apparent task of KOA: *content selection* now shifts into the background, becoming a backstage activity: KBA: *content selection*, effectively hidden from the customer's view.

From Support to Backstage (KSA >KBA)

Shifting activities from support to backstage involves transforming functions that were previously only tangentially involved in the value creation process into core activities that directly contribute to it. A notable example is the pervasive use of social media in digital marketing strategies, which has led to an increased reliance on analytics software tools such as Hootsuite, Google Analytics, and Buffer. These tools are employed to track the performance of advertising campaigns across the most popular social media platforms. Initially, these analytics services played a supporting role for social network companies, indirectly enhancing their value creation process by attracting more users for professional purposes. Recognizing the pivotal role of data collection and analysis in their business models, many social media giants have ventured into providing their own analytics services, exemplified by Facebook Analytics. This transformation signifies a paradigm shift where what was once considered a—KSA: *data collection and analysis*—now turns into a KBA, paving the way for the development of new business models with a professional orientation (e.g., Facebook for Business).

From Backstage to Support (KBA >KSA)

Certain activities can be reclassified as support activities, signifying that they now serve the value creation process only indirectly. Consider the e-commerce revolution and the increasing integration of offline and online shopping experiences. Fast fashion giants such as Zara and H&M have implemented a system allowing customers to purchase items online and retrieve them directly from a physical store, eliminating the need to wait for home delivery. This streamlined approach also extends to returns, which can be conveniently processed at the nearest store for an immediate refund.

In this scenario, the KBA *retailer management* shifts to being a support activity (KSA) role, providing indirect but crucial support to enhance the online shopping experience.

Switching by Changing the Key Actors

Another method of switching the *roles* entails reassigning responsibility for specific key activities to different actors, including the company, partners, and customers. Here are a few examples of *switching by changing the roles*.

Company to Customers and Vice Versa

Take, for instance, McDonald's recent introduction of "totems"— kiosks resembling oversized smartphones positioned inside restaurants, where customers can place their orders without waiting in line at the counter. In this scenario, the customer takes on a key new activity: *managing orders*, a task previously handled by the company. This switch not only enhances the customer experience but also innovates the business model in two significant ways. First, the consumer has plenty of time to browse the menu and customize their order. Second, with employees freed from the tasks of order processing and cash handling, they can now focus on delivering food to tables, undertaking a key activity that was once the customer's responsibility—*food serving*.

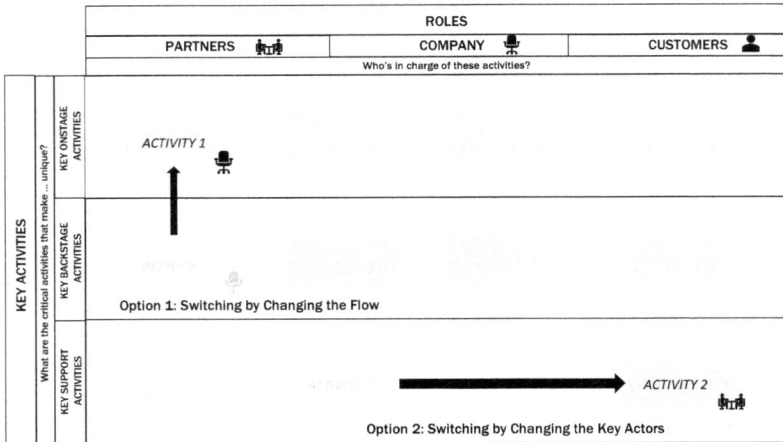

Figure 4.5 Approaches to switching the roles

Company to Partners and Vice Versa

Imagine a company (let's call it *TechSolutions*) that provides a suite of software products and services to businesses. Traditionally, *TechSolutions* handles all aspects of product development, implementation, and customer support. Now, let's explore a switching scenario: *TechSolutions* could decide to open up its platform and collaborate with a network of partners, including independent developers, consultants, and industry experts. Instead of solely relying on in-house expertise, *TechSolutions* actively involves these partners in the *development and customization of their solutions*. This empowers partners to contribute their specialized knowledge and skills to create a more diverse and tailored suite of products and services. In return, *TechSolutions* could pivot to focus on platform governance, quality assurance, and providing robust tools and resources to support its partners. This new role involves setting standards, ensuring compatibility, and fostering a collaborative environment within the ecosystem. As a result of this *switching*, *TechSolutions* undergoes a fundamental transformation in its business model. Instead of being a standalone software provider, it evolves into a platform enabler that orchestrates a dynamic ecosystem of partners, each adding unique value to the offerings.

Key Takeaways

In summary, transforming the BML by switching the roles entails two alternative approaches:

1. **Switching by Changing the Flow of Activities:**
   - Shifting from onstage to backstage activities
   - Transitioning from backstage to onstage activities
   - Moving from support to backstage activities
2. **Switching by Changing the Key Actors:**
   - Interchanging roles between the company and customers
   - Interchanging roles between the company and partners

   By implementing any of these operations, you have the opportunity to redefine and restructure the original roles, ultimately leading to a comprehensive transformation of the entire BML.

Business Case Example

Switching the roles for a more sustainable consumption: The Splosh one-sale approach

With the ultimate mission of reducing plastic waste, in 2012, the eco-conscious entrepreneur Angus Graham launched Splosh, an innovative e-commerce platform for household products. Splosh offers a unique approach to sustainable consumption, allowing customers to purchase refillable household cleaning and personal care products. This contrasts with the conventional practice of buying new bottles filled with products on a weekly basis. Upon initial sign-up, customers invest in a one-off starter box. This box contains elegantly designed bottles and pouches filled with concentrated liquid. These can be easily diluted with tap water, creating usable products such as detergent, washing-up liquid, and shower gel. When a product runs out, the customer receives new sachets of concentrated liquid to refill the previously provided bottles. Furthermore, once the pouches are depleted, customers have the option to return them to the company for recycling.

This unique approach innovates the business model for household cleaning products by switching the roles. It involved a fundamental shift in activity flow and introduced new roles for customers. In this reimagined model, customers actively participate in the product realization process (such as concentrate dilution and bottle refilling) and engage in recycling activities by sending pouches back to the company. Conversely, activities that held significance in the traditional model, such as large-scale distribution, have become irrelevant. As a result, partner retailers have been relieved of their previous functions, which have been seamlessly taken over by shipping companies responsible for delivering products directly to consumers' doorsteps. This transformational shift in roles led to significant changes in other BML elements, including meaning (people buy Splosh products to clean their house while being sustainable), key resources (packaging design is not relevant anymore), and several aspects of the performance (for example, delivery boxes designed to fit through a letterbox).

Chapter Overview

This chapter focuses on the fourth element of the BML: *roles*. This encompasses the identification of key activities, understanding their flow in value creation, and determining the responsible parties. When analyzing and designing *roles*, a three-step approach is employed: first, the identification of key activities; next, categorizing them into onstage, backstage, and support activities to map their flow; finally, establishing accountability for each key activity (key actor) among the company, partners, or customers. *Roles* can be reshaped through a collaborative practice, achieved through two alternative approaches: switching by altering the flow of activities and switching by changing the key actors. Implementing either of these operations presents an opportunity to redefine and restructure the original *roles*, ultimately leading to a comprehensive transformation of the entire BML.

CHAPTER 5

Swapping the Value Equation

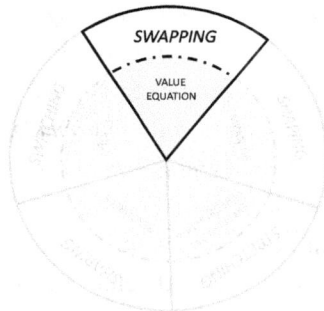

Figure 5.1 Swapping the value equation

What Will You Learn?

You will:

- Understand, in a Business Model Logic (BML), which aspects define the value equation.
- Learn how to analyze the value equation in a BML.
- Learn how to design the value equation in your BML practically.
- Understand how to trigger a BML transformation by swapping the value equation.
- Understand the implications of swapping the value equation in a BML from real-world business examples (Figure 5.1).

Element #5 Value Equation: No Pain, No Gain

Value-first is a perception. If your customer does not perceive it as value, then it's not very valuable

—Jeffrey Gitomer

When Nespresso launched their widely popular campaign featuring the charismatic George Clooney, leisurely sipping espresso in glamorous settings, the focus was primarily on the luxurious experience rather than the innovative, albeit expensive, coffee-making system that revolutionized the in-home coffee market. With the simple tagline "Nespresso … what else?," the campaign positioned Nespresso as a choice synonymous with exclusivity, catering to coffee *aficionados* seeking the pinnacle of quality without necessarily going into the technical specifics of its value offer. Thanks to meticulously designed capsules, presented in elegant packaging akin to precious chocolates, Nespresso claims to have garnered seven million devoted "club members." These members regularly receive shipments of aluminum capsules, investing individually between £119 and £449 in each machine. This loyalty endures despite the abundance of more budget-friendly alternatives available in the market. Ultimately, consumers don't purchase products or services solely for their features but as a means to attain specific benefits. This concept, viewing a product as a *bundle of benefits*, has its roots in a decades-old principle. It posits that a product is not merely a set of features but a collection of benefit and advantages it delivers to the consumer. From a customer's perspective, these benefits can be functional, emotional, or relational in nature. Functional benefits encompass tangible, utilitarian advantages such as time-saving, enhanced performance, or heightened convenience. Emotional benefits entail the positive feelings or experiences associated with the product, such as joy, comfort, or relief. Relational benefits refer to the product's impact on social interactions or status.

Considering a product as a bundle of benefits offers a deeper understanding of the value it provides from the customer's perspective. This insight serves as a foundation for crafting robust value propositions and enhancing overall customer satisfaction. However, a complete customer perspective also requires considering the costs and effort involved in getting a specific product or service. Costs represent the sacrifices, expenses, or efforts of acquiring, using, or maintaining a product or service. These can include monetary efforts (e.g., purchase price, ongoing expenses), time efforts (e.g., time spent researching, learning, or using the product), and psychophysical efforts (e.g., physical or mental exertion). In addition to a clear picture of our products' benefits, having a better sense of what the customer perceives as an effort is essential to determining pricing strategies, enhancing value proposition, gaining a competitive advantage, allocating resources efficiently, ensuring operating cost-effectively, and driving continuous improvement. So, what do customers perceive as the benefits of your product? And what efforts are they willing to invest to gain those benefits? These questions underpin the final element of the BML: the *value equation*. This principle, introduced as a cornerstone of marketing, quantifies the disparity between a consumer's perceived benefits and the total perceived efforts required to attain them (Value = Benefits/Efforts). It serves as the fundamental evaluation that customers make before making a purchase or comparing similar offerings.

Thus, designing a BML necessitates unbundling and defining the benefits and efforts deemed relevant by customers concerning the core product or service. However, in the last years, particularly among younger generations, there has been an increased awareness of benefits and efforts that extend beyond individual needs. Customers increasingly choose brands aligning with their values, considering broader impacts on society and the environment. Social media exposure fuels debates about sustainability and inclusivity, leading to greater levels of awareness about the practices adopted by companies in these domains.

As a consequence, there has been a proliferation of conscious brands, and sustainability has become a powerful marketing leverage for many companies. The reality is that no matter how a product or service performs well, companies can no longer ignore the inclusion of sustainability and inclusivity aspects in their practices, not only for regulatory compliance but also for market relevance. As a result, the value equation of companies is increasingly enriched by society- and environment-related dimensions that go beyond consumers' mere personal utility, prioritizing transparency in their supply chains, the use of sustainable materials, and promoting fair labor practices. For example, brands like Patagonia have gained popularity not only for their high-quality outdoor apparel but also for their commitment to environmental and social responsibility. Their campaigns, such as "Don't Buy This Jacket," encourage consumers to think twice about consumption and promote a more sustainable approach to fashion. Consumers who choose Patagonia are not just purchasing clothing; they are aligning themselves with a brand that values environmental conservation and ethical sourcing. The functional benefits of durable and well-designed clothing are coupled with emotional benefits tied to supporting a company with a strong social and environmental conscience. On the other hand, customers' perceived efforts, such as premium pricing or a narrower product variety, are deemed acceptable as long as customers are satisfied with the broader impact of their choices.

In conclusion, value must be perceived through the customer's lens, emerging from the interplay between perceived benefits and efforts. When designing a BML, ensuring this balance favors the customer—where benefits outweigh efforts—is crucial. Simultaneously, from a business standpoint, the value equation should be structured to not only deliver value but also enable the business to capture a portion of that value through an appropriate pricing strategy, covering costs and ensuring profitability for long-term sustainability.

Wrap-Up Questions

In essence, the value equation in the BML can be defined by two basic questions:

1. What benefits do users gain from a specific product or service?
2. What efforts are demanded from users to acquire a specific product or service?

Warm-Up Task

1. Select a successful product or service you are familiar with. Outline at least three benefits that you find significant for the customer. These benefits can encompass personal utility, and the perceived positive impact of the product or service on the environment and society.

Brand/Product:_____

a._____

b._____

c._____

d._____

e._____

2. Now, consider at least three efforts that you think the customer needs to undertake in association with the consumption of the product/service you mentioned. These efforts can encompass personal utility and the perceived negative impact of the product or service on the environment and society.

a._____

b._____

c._____

d._____

e._____

Understanding the Value Equation

In the earlier section of this chapter, we introduced the fifth element of the BML: the value equation, emphasizing the interplay between consumer, societal, and environmental perspectives. It revolves around two pivotal questions: What benefits do users derive from a specific product or service, and what efforts are expected from users to obtain it? To systematically analyze and design a product or service's value equation, employ a user-friendly tool that breaks down the value equation design process into three straightforward steps:

- **Step 1. Assess the Benefits Provided**: This involves dissecting the offering into tangible and intangible benefits that hold relevance for the customers.
- **Step 2. Assess Required Effort:** Understand the specific pain points that customers may encounter throughout their experience.
- **Step 3. Evaluate the Value Delivered:** This step aims to ascertain if the perceived benefits in your value equation outweigh the perceived efforts. It enables you to determine whether genuine value is being created for your customer (Figure 5.2).

Step 1 . Assess the Benefits Provided

During this stage, your focus should be on understanding the functional, emotional, and relational *benefits* that customers perceive based on their individual needs. To conduct a thorough analysis of the value equation, it is crucial to recognize that customer benefits extend beyond their individual utility sphere and encompass broader societal and environmental dimensions. This recognition is pivotal for designing a value equation that not only meets immediate customer needs but also aligns with contemporary expectations and sustainability goals.

Given the diverse nature of consumer priorities, addressing each customer segment with a tailored value equation is preferable. Consider the following perspectives.

Customer-Related Benefits

Assess how the value offering helps customers in:

- Accomplishing Tasks: Evaluate how the product or service aids users in functional, social, or emotional tasks and activities in their personal or professional lives (e.g., writing a report or maintaining a healthy lifestyle).

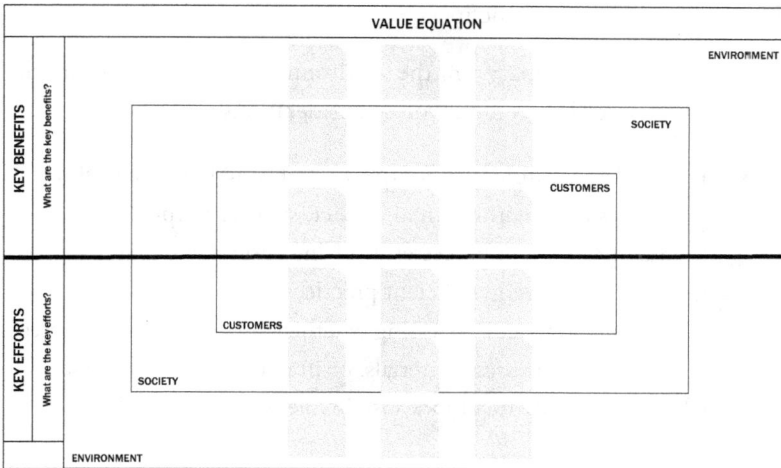

Figure 5.2 Value equation subdimensions

- Obtaining Desired Results: Explore how the offering provides
  results and benefits, such as improved performance, enhanced
  design, or increased comfort.
- Mitigating Obstacles or Risks: Identify how the product or
  service helps users overcome obstacles or risks associated with
  specific tasks, providing solutions that save time, money, and
  effort.

Society-Related Benefits

Examine the product or service's contribution to societal well-being.
This may encompass:

- Social Responsibility: Assessing how the business engages in
  social causes or community development. This might involve
  charity contributions, partnerships with community organizations, or initiatives promoting societal well-being.
- Ethical Considerations: Assessing how the offering aligns with
  ethical standards or fair practices.

Environment-Related Benefits

Assess the positive impact on the environment stemming from the product or service. This could involve considerations such as:

- Reduced Environmental Footprint: Assessing how the business minimizes the environmental impact, such as adopting eco-friendly production processes, utilizing sustainable materials, or implementing energy-efficient practices.
- Sustainable Practices: Assessing whether the service incorporates eco-friendly processes, materials, or practices, and how these efforts contribute to a more sustainable business model.

Returning to the example of *Compasses Magazine*, which focuses on architecture and design in the Middle East, let's consider the perceived customer-, society-, and environment-related benefits perceived by their professional customer segment (architects and designers) (Figure 5.3).

For this group, the magazine's customer-related benefits lie in functional benefits that facilitate their task completion (such as providing interior design consultancies). It also addresses pain points and enhances gains associated with each task, including *"access to curated, high-quality content,"* edited by a team of experts in the field, which leads to more original projects (a gain creator) while reducing time spent on research and travel for inspiration (a pain reliever). Furthermore, the *"availability in multiple formats,"* whether digital or printed, enables customers to access the magazine in various situations, such as while traveling, thereby overcoming constraints such as limited time and space preventing their research *job* from being done. Other benefits may include the *"feeling of becoming acknowledged in a specific field"* or the *"sense of belonging to a community of urban design and architecture enthusiasts,"* which relate more to the emotional and relational sphere of the customer.

As for the society-related benefits, the magazine's *"commitment to showcasing the work of emerging designers and architects"* contributes to inclusion within the professional community. It serves as a platform that acknowledges their expertise, fostering a sense of professional acknowledgment and community belonging. Finally, regarding environment-related benefits, these include *"sustainable printing practices,"* such as the use of recycled paper or the *"provision of digital formats,"* which contribute to a reduced environmental footprint and align with contemporary expectations for environmentally conscious business operations, as well as the promotion of eco-design products and architectural principles that educate readers toward more sustainable decorating and building practices.

Step 2. Assess Required Effort

The second step involves identifying the *efforts* that customers associate with our product or service. As mentioned earlier, these efforts can stem from various sources, encompassing the customer's individual utility, as well as broader societal and environmental dimensions.

Customer-Related Efforts

One effective approach to identify customers' perceived efforts is to scrutinize their potential journey in relation to the consumption of the target product or service. This entails identifying specific pain points that customers encounter while accessing and consuming a specific product or service. These pain points signify moments or interactions where customers face difficulties, frustrations, or challenges. These efforts may include the following:

- Monetary effort refers to the price paid for a product or service, along with any related costs for its use. This includes unexpected or hidden costs, which can create a gap between the perceived value and the actual financial investment required.
- Time effort refers to the time spent before or during the use of a product or service. This includes long waits during purchase, use, or maintenance, which can cause customer frustration and lower satisfaction.
- Psychophysical effort refers to the physical or mental effort needed before or during the use of a product or service.

Complex setup procedures, confusing interfaces, or a lack of user-friendly features can increase the effort required, reducing overall satisfaction.

Society-Related Efforts

Consider the negative impact of the product or service that might negatively affect societal well-being, taking into account the customer's viewpoint. For instance, a product that induces addictive behaviors or reinforces detrimental stereotypes. Additionally, society-related efforts could extend beyond the immediate product impact to encompass a broader corporate context, such as the company's engagement in discriminatory practices or implementation of unethical labor policies.

Environment-Related Efforts

Assess the potential negative impact of the product or service on the environment, particularly through the lens of the customer. For instance, this involves evaluating whether the offering incorporates environmentally harmful processes and materials, such as excessive use of polluting packaging or the nondisposability of products. Additionally, when addressing environmental efforts, considerations may include broader aspects of the company's environmental practices, such as the lack of eco-friendly initiatives, which result in a larger environmental footprint due to resource-intensive production, wasteful processes, or the use of non-sustainable materials.

Returning to the example of *Compasses Magazine*, which focuses on architecture and design in the Middle East, let's consider the perceived customer-, society-, and environmental-related efforts perceived by their professional customer segment—architects and designers (Figure 5.3).

For example, in the case of Compasses Magazine, the primary customer-related efforts might include:

- *Purchasing Cost*: Customers invest money in acquiring the magazine, be it through a subscription or a one-time purchase.

- *Additional Expenses*: There might be supplementary costs for purchasing design materials, tools, or products recommended or featured in the magazine.
- *Cognitive Load*: Customers exert mental energy in comprehending the magazine's content. This encompasses understanding technical terminology, grasping design concepts, and analyzing visual representations.
- *Further Research*: Customers may devote additional time researching topics or projects mentioned in the magazine, seeking more details or exploring related resources and references.

For societal efforts, potential concerns might include a lack of gender representation on the editorial board, which could affect the magazine's societal inclusiveness. Additionally, promoting products made from non-sustainable materials without addressing their environmental impact could be seen as an environment-related effort.

It's important to recognize that the level of effort in each category can vary depending on factors like content complexity, the reader's familiarity with the topic, and personal preferences. Therefore, just like with benefits, categorizing customer efforts should be customized for each targeted segment.

Step 3. Evaluate the Value Delivered

As a final step, compare the efforts that customers undertake (as identified in Step 2) to the value they receive (as identified in Step 1) from the product or service at the core of your BML. This can be done by creating a detailed *value equation* with efforts as the denominator and benefits as the numerator. Break it down into layers, examining customer-, society-, and environmental-related benefits and efforts. Visualizing the value equation will help you better assess whether the product or service provides sufficient benefits that justify the customers' investment of money, time, ethical compromises, and environmental impact. Use the value equation to visualize the dynamics between customer efforts and the derived value. Understand if the overall balance is in equilibrium or if adjustments are needed. This evaluation serves as a diagnostic tool, pinpointing areas where the effort–value balance can be enhanced. Prioritize these opportunities for a change to refine aspects that contribute to a more compelling and satisfying customer experience.

So What?

Identifying customer benefits and efforts in the value equation serves as a foundation for a BML transformation. By integrating customer needs with societal and environmental dimensions, the value equation goes beyond functionality, enhancing the overall customer experience and aligning with contemporary expectations and sustainability goals. This approach ensures that offerings meet immediate customer needs while addressing broader societal expectations. By identifying the benefits and efforts your customers perceive in the value equation, you can gain a deeper understanding of their needs and identify areas that need improvement to be used as a starting point for a BML transformation.

TST Challenge

Analyzing the Value Equation: Uber for Women (Aged 18 to 35)
To gain insights into the value equation for our specific customer segment (women aged 18 to 35) within the context of Uber*, identify their jobs, pains, and gains by using the following diagram.

Customer segment pains: _____

Customer segment gains: _____

---

*Uber is a pioneering ride-sharing platform that has transformed urban transportation. Through a user-friendly mobile app, Uber seamlessly connects passengers with nearby drivers, offering a hassle-free and convenient way to get around cities. With a range of vehicle options spanning from cost-effective to premium, Uber provides flexibility to cater to various customer preferences. The platform's emphasis on safety and real-time tracking has made it a trusted and go-to solution for millions of users seeking reliable and comfortable transportation worldwide (www.uber.com/).

Design Tips

Visualizing the identified benefits and efforts can enhance clarity. Imagine placing each benefit on a separate sticky note and organizing them into horizontal rows categorized by customer-related, society-related, and environment-related benefits. Draw a line underneath to create a clear separation. Then, place each corresponding effort on a sticky note below the benefits, using distinct levels for customer, society, or environment-related efforts. This visual method aids in comprehensive analysis, making it easier to understand the significance of each benefit and effort in relation to your product or service.

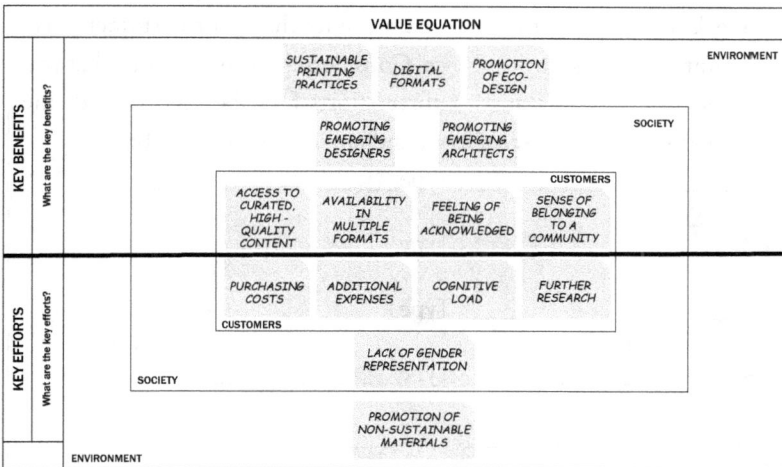

Figure 5.3 Compasses value equation

Customer jobs: _____

Step 1. Assess the Benefits Provided

Considering the customer segments' jobs, pains, and gains, name at least three benefits that Uber provides them and then define their nature (customer-, society-, and environment-related).

B1. _____; Type_____

B2. _____; Type_____

B3. _____; Type_____

B4. _____; Type_____

B5. _____; Type_____

Step 2. Assess the Required Effort

Now, imagine the customer journey for your customer segment while using Uber. Identify the main pain points that your customers may encounter while using the service. Considering the pain points that you have identified, name at least three efforts for Uber and then define their nature (customer-, society-, and environment-related).

E1. _____; Type_____

E2. _____; Type_____

E3. _____; Type_____

E4. _____; Type_____

E5. _____; Type_____

Step 3. Evaluate the Value Delivered

Place the benefits identified above the line. Then, place the efforts below. Use the different frameworks' layers to place benefits and efforts according to their nature. Think about how benefits and efforts are balanced. Use the template provided (Figure 5.4).

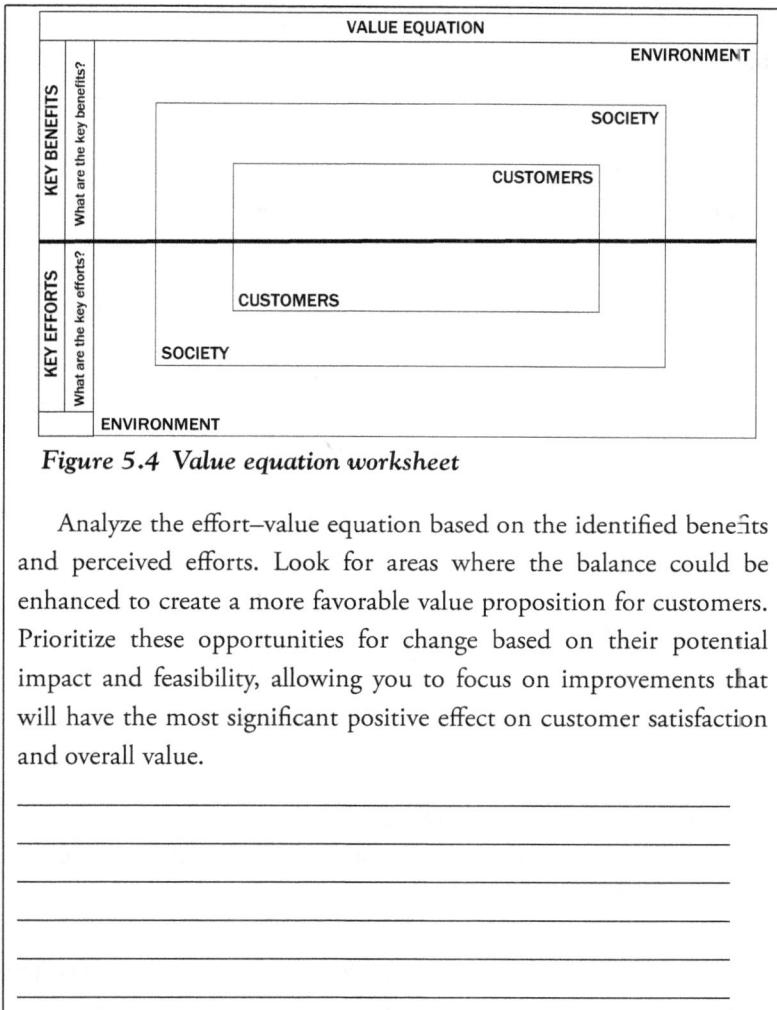

Figure 5.4 Value equation worksheet

Analyze the effort–value equation based on the identified benefits and perceived efforts. Look for areas where the balance could be enhanced to create a more favorable value proposition for customers. Prioritize these opportunities for change based on their potential impact and feasibility, allowing you to focus on improvements that will have the most significant positive effect on customer satisfaction and overall value.

_____
_____
_____
_____
_____
_____

TST Practice #5 Transforming the Business Model Logic by Swapping the Value Equation

The last BML transformational practice is *swapping*, which can be defined as the process of redesigning the value equation by modifying or reversing the set of benefits (B1, ..., Bn) and efforts (E1, ..., En) as perceived by the customer. After having identified the set of benefits (Step 1) and efforts (Step 2) for the segment of interest and having assessed the effort–value balance (Step 3), you can start thinking about which areas of the value equation can be improved by leveraging on the different benefits and efforts. The redefinition of the value equation will lead you to experiment with alternative business model transformations by *swapping* the *value equation*, which can be approached in the following two ways:

Remove and Add Benefits/Efforts

First, you can swap your value equation by removing and adding one or more new efforts and benefits across the different levels of the current value equation. Let's take, for example, one of the most common chores in our everyday life: grocery shopping. While some find it a therapeutic exercise, meticulously checking off items on their neatly organized lists, others may feel overwhelmed navigating aisles filled with plenty of products, feeling absolutely lost while having to decide between chopped tomatoes, diced tomatoes, tomato paste, marinara, or pasta sauce to cook a simple dish of spaghetti. Broadly speaking, the value equation of a typical large food retail business model has some crosscutting (customer-level benefit) benefits, including, for example:

- *Wide product range:* including groceries, household items, personal care products, and so on, streamlining the shopping experience and saving time;
- *Convenience and accessibility:* as strategic locations with extended operating hours and parking spaces that allow shoppers to visit at their convenience;
- *Self-service format:* allowing customers to browse and select products themselves and make informed decisions;
- *Competitive pricing:* such as low prices and frequent promotions for cost savings.

However, these customer-level benefits may be offset by challenges such as coping with crowded spaces, the absence of personal assistance, or the risk of unplanned purchases (customer-level efforts). Additionally, there are broader societal and environmental efforts to consider. Large supermarkets might lead to the relocation of smaller local businesses, affecting communities and causing economic challenges (society-level effort). Some grocery stores may worsen environmental issues with excessive non-recyclable packaging, contributing to pollution and plastic waste (environment-level effort). Poor waste management, like improper food waste disposal or inadequate recycling programs, can also harm the environment (environment-level effort). This can be especially concerning for those individuals who are particularly sensitive to the environmental impact of their purchases, leading them to seek more eco-friendly alternatives. With this in mind and inspired by the wave of the subscription-based models, in 2012, Matt Salzberg, Ilia Papas, and Matt Wadiak founded *Blue Apron* in New York City. *Blue Apron* is a subscription meal kit service that delivers preportioned ingredients and recipes directly to customers' homes. Subscribers can choose from various weekly recipes and receive the necessary ingredients and step-by-step instructions to prepare meals. Thanks to its success, *Blue Apron* paved the way for adopting the subscription box business model in the grocery market, which led to a shift in the traditional grocery market's *value equation*. The once-existing effort of *lack of personal assistance and guidance* is eliminated, sparing customers the stress of *product selection*. Instead, the service adopts the role of a personal shopper, curating selections based on specific themes or preferences. In particular, this last benefit could be a real solution for those who lack the time or food knowledge to make informed decisions or who are simply too lazy to meticulously plan their meals. This approach not only introduces the benefit of discovering new products but also adds an element of surprise as subscribers anticipate the unique contents of each box. Beyond eliminating the customer-level efforts associated with product selection and lack of personal assistance, *Blue Apron* introduces significant environment- and society-related benefits. The model reduces the environmental footprint by delivering preportioned ingredients, minimizing food waste compared to traditional grocery shopping—a boon for environmentally conscious individuals seeking sustainable alternatives. Additionally, the service's curated selections reduce unplanned purchases, encouraging more mindful consumption.

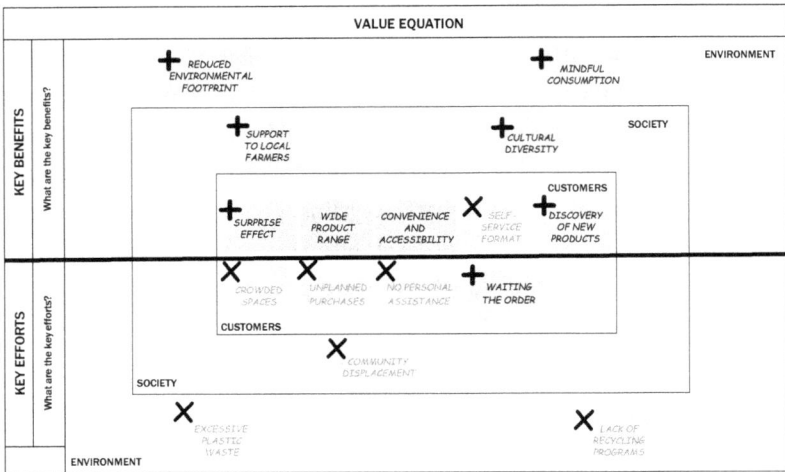

Figure 5.5 Swapping by removing and adding benefits/efforts

At the societal level, *Blue Apron* fosters a sense of community by supporting local farmers and artisans through responsible sourcing, stimulating local economies, and ensuring that customers are part of a broader, more sustainable food ecosystem. The subscription model encourages diverse culinary exploration, celebrating cultural diversity with various international recipes and ingredients.

In summary, *Blue Apron*'s subscription box model not only streamlines the individual shopping experience but also introduces significant environmental and societal benefits. It effectively addresses the growing demand for sustainable and community-oriented practices in the grocery market, presenting a holistic solution for individuals seeking a more conscious approach to their daily habits (Figure 5.5).

Reverse Benefits and Efforts

As a second option, you can swap your value equation by reversing benefits with efforts and vice versa across its different levels. The freemium business model revolution can help us to understand this approach better. Let's take, for example, the value equation of iTunes when it was first introduced in 2001, which revolutionized how music was bought and consumed digitally.

In the original business model, iTunes' value equation included several customer-related benefits, such as:

- *Individual song purchase*: The possibility to buy specific songs without having to invest in the entire album;
- *Extensive music catalog*: The provision of a comprehensive collection of music across different genres, artists, and record labels, which represented an easy way to discover new music;
- *Personalization and organization*: The possibility to organize music in libraries, create playlists, and customize the listening experience;
- *Integration with Apple ecosystem*: The possibility to automatically sync the music library on multiple devices (Mac, iPod, iPhone, and iPad) and enjoy the music on the go.

On the other hand, these benefits are offset by some efforts, such as:

- *Financial burden*: The standardized pricing of $0.99 was still perceived as a considerable monetary effort for an intangible product, potentially hindering their ability to access and enjoy a broad range of digital music.
- *Time and effort in music selection*: Users had to explore and browse through the vast catalog actively to find music aligned with their tastes and preferences;
- *Complex syncing and device management*: The need for users to connect devices, manage storage, and handle file transfers adds complexity and effort to the user experience, potentially discouraging less tech-savvy individuals.

Moreover, there were broader societal efforts to consider, such as the potential exclusivity and digital divide. The purchasing cost and the necessity for compatible devices might contribute to a digital divide, creating exclusivity and limiting access to legal digital music for individuals with lower resources.

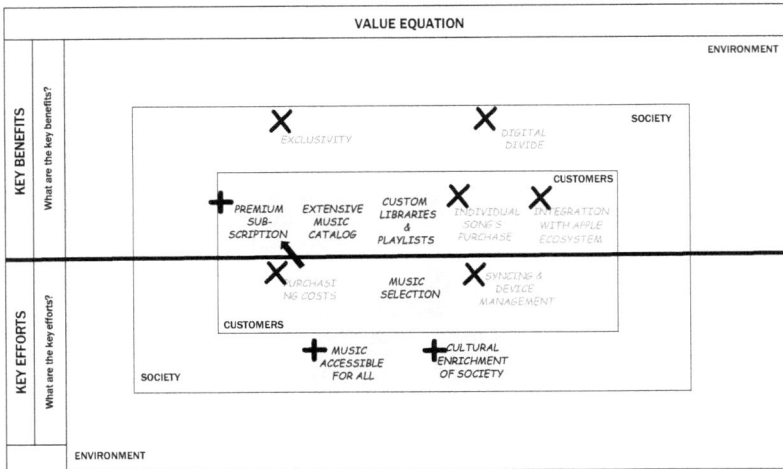

Figure 5.6 Swapping by reversing benefits/efforts

In 2007, when Daniel Ek and Martin Lorentzon started to design the business model of Spotify, they were obsessed with one idea in particular: music had to be freely accessible to all. Owing to the widespread diffusion of piracy music and illegal downloading platforms at the time, people seemed no longer willing to bear any monetary efforts related to the acquisition of music. Spotify's founders had the idea to make this wish not only come true but even legal, by planning to buy licenses from music labels and rely on sponsorships to give users free access to an unlimited catalog of music. However, relying solely on sponsorship for revenue may not have provided a consistent and reliable income stream to support the operations and growth of Spotify. Therefore, they decided to adopt a freemium model where the free tier granted users access to the platform and streaming for free, albeit with occasional advertisements and some limitations. The premium tier, available for a monthly fee, offered ad-free listening, higher audio quality, and the ability to download music for offline enjoyment.

Although the early intention to completely eliminate the monetary effort in the value equation of digital music companies (such as iTunes) seemed unviable, Spotify's innovative approach reversed the monetary effort into a perceived benefit. Users did not view the monetary contribution as an obligation, as they could still enjoy the unlimited music catalog for free. The option to upgrade to the premium subscription was perceived as an additional benefit, providing an enhanced user experience and fostering a sense of community among music enthusiasts.

This shift in approach not only eliminated society-level efforts associated with exclusivity and the digital divide, as perceived in the original iTunes model, but also transformed them into society-level benefits. Spotify's freemium model contributed to the accessibility and inclusivity of legal, free music consumption, thus contributing to the cultural enrichment of society (Figure 5.6).

Key Takeaways

To sum up, to transform the BML by swapping, you can modify the value equation, that is, the set of benefits and efforts the customer perceives in relation to the value offerings purchased. Specifically, the value equation can be swapped by:

1. Removing and adding one or more new efforts and benefits across various levels, encompassing customer experience, societal impact, and environmental considerations;
2. Reversing benefits with efforts and vice versa within the current value equation across its different levels.

By performing one of these two operations, you can redefine the original value equation. This, in turn, will trigger a transformation of the whole BML of your value offering.

Business Case Example

H&M Rewear: From Fast-Fashion to Second-Hand

Founded in 1947 in Sweden, H&M—short for Hennes and Mauritz—established itself as a pioneering company in offering trendy clothing at affordable prices. In the 1970s, the company expanded beyond Sweden and opened its first international store in Norway. Later on, through strategic acquisitions and a commitment to meeting customer needs, H&M has grown into a global fashion powerhouse with retail stores across all of Europe and worldwide.

With a business model focused on offering a wide range of fashionable items at cheap prices, with frequent inventory turnover, H&M was one of the first companies to introduce the fast-fashion model as we know it today. From a customer perspective, the value equation of a fast-fashion company is undoubtedly appealing. First of all, they make fashion accessible, as most items replicate the latest trends seen on the catwalks but at affordable prices. As a second benefit, there is an immense variety of products that allow customers to find everything they may need, including outwear, underwear, sportswear, and so on, in one single store. Finally, the shopping experience, thanks to a convenient store layout, self-service, and accessible product displays, allows the customer to browse and select items without the pressure to buy independently. Obviously, there are downsides. Typical efforts for the customer concern primarily the low quality and low durability of items, as fast-fashion usually prioritizes low prices and quick turnover. Secondly, the lack of personal assistance, the size of the stores, and the long queues at the changing rooms or checkouts can sometimes make the shopping experience quite stressful. Additionally, in the last years, the fast-fashion business model has faced severe criticism for its environmental and social impacts, including issues related to sustainability, ethical production practices, and labor conditions that were giving customers the feeling of doing something bad for the planet. This last point led to additional society- and environment-related efforts, especially for the younger generation, who proved to be particularly sensitive to ethical and waste concerns. H&M was one of the first players in the market to take a step to address this issue by launching a new business model—H&M Rewear—a second-hand consumer-to-consumer (C2C) platform. Initially launched specifically for the Canadian market, H&M Rewear is a digital store where customers can resell their clothes in exchange for direct deposit or an H&M gift card with an added 20 percent value that can be reclaimed at H&M online and in-store.

By leveraging on a specific effort of the value equation, that is, the feeling of doing something bad for the planet, H&M has been able to reverse it into a benefit by creating a brand new second-hand business model that gives the customer the feeling of being environmentally responsible by limiting overproduction and overconsumption.

Chapter Overview

In this chapter, we defined the fifth element of the BML, the *value equation*. It includes hypotheses about the set of benefits and efforts as perceived by the customer in association with a specific product or service. The *value equation* for a business can be analyzed and designed through a three-step process. First, identify the key benefits for each customer segment recognizing those benefits beyond their individual utility sphere and encompass broader societal and environmental dimensions. Then, formulate hypotheses about the perceived efforts customers need to put in to obtain those benefits, taking in due account the customer-, society-, and environment-related dimensions. Finally, identify areas where the effort–value balance can be improved and prioritize opportunities for change. Finally, we illustrated the fifth BML transformational practice, *swapping*. A *swapping* transformation can be defined as the process of modifying and redesigning the value equation of the BML This can involve the removal or addition of existing benefits or efforts. Alternatively, a *swapping* transformation can be achieved by reversing the roles of efforts and benefits in the current value equation.

CHAPTER 6

Disruptive Innovations

What Will You Learn in This Chapter?

You will:

- Understand which aspects define a disruptive innovation.
- Learn how disruptive innovation can affect a business model logic.
- Understand how to deal with a disruptive innovation by using the TST.
- Understand the implications of adopting a TST in the face of disruptive innovation from a real-world business case.

Challenge #1 Disruptive Innovation: From the Fringe to the Mainstream

The term *disruptive* was first applied to innovation in 1997 in the pages of *The Innovator's Dilemma*, one of the most influential business books of the 21st century, authored by Clayton Christensen, professor at Harvard Business School.

In his book, Christensen defines *disruptive innovation* as an innovation capable of transforming an industry or market by introducing a new product, service, technology, or business model that disrupts existing businesses, jeopardizing the competitive advantage of established companies. To be more specific, what sets disruptive innovation apart from—for example—breakthrough innovations is their origin and progression. Unlike breakthrough innovations, often associated with particular products, services, or technologies, disruptive innovations are better defined as *processes* that transform costly and complex offerings into more affordable and accessible alternatives so more people can use them.

Take the first automobiles in the late 19th century, for example. They weren't disruptive because they were expensive and complex luxuries for rich people, which did not perturb the market for horse-drawn vehicles. This equilibrium in the transportation market remained until a forward-thinking entrepreneur named Henry Ford decided to lock in the design of the popular Model T. He reduced the car-building time from 12 to 2.5 h. This move let him shrink the costs even more, drop the prices, and drive the growth of Ford Motor Company from 10,000 cars manufactured in 1908 to 472,350 cars in 1915 to 933,720 cars in 1920. The Ford Model T became the first mass-produced car affordable for a broad range of consumers, and its production set the stage for modern manufacturing processes. That's when cars finally disrupted the transportation systems, changing cities' urban planning and dynamics, sparkling new businesses, such as gas stations and repair shops, and influencing industries such as oil production and road construction.

Another distinctive aspect of disruptive innovation is that it frequently originates from outsiders and entrepreneurial start-ups rather than well-established industry leaders. Indeed, disruptive innovations usually set their sights on the more affordable market segment or work toward engaging nonconsumers who are currently unserved with suitable alternatives. Through this approach, disruptive innovation shows a progression wherein a product or service initially gains traction through straightforward applications at the lower end of the market—often by being more budget-friendly and easier to access—and then gradually advances into higher tiers of the market, eventually displacing established competitors. Now, why don't the big players jump on these game-changing ideas right away? Well, the hesitation is often due to the fact that these innovations might not immediately generate substantial profits, and their development could divert valuable resources away from sustaining innovations—the kind they feel needed to compete against their rivals.

However, established companies' myopia for disruption innovations is one of the most common mistakes in the business history of epic failures. One popular example can be found in the home entertainment market.

Picture a time when people lined up at Blockbuster stores, eagerly eyeing rows of DVDs for their weekend entertainment fix. Blockbuster held the throne confident in its model of physical rental and late fees with over 9,000 video rental stores globally and 85,000 employees worldwide. Yet, beneath the surface, a revolution was brewing. Enter Netflix, a scrappy newcomer with an innovative idea: mail-order DVD rentals. It was the beginning of the 2000s, and Netflix's mail-in movie subscription service didn't catch the eye of Blockbuster's mainstream clients; instead, it resonated with tech-savvy early adopters already familiar with online shopping. In the face of Blockbuster's towering success, Netflix lacked the resources and ambition to confront the behemoth head-on. Blinded by its achievements, Blockbuster dismissed the new business concept brought up by Netflix as trivial, overlooking the seeds of disruption that were being sown. But, the story doesn't end there. Netflix recognized an untapped segment at the lower end of the market—where simplicity and cost-effectiveness reigned supreme. As technology advances, Netflix transforms into a digital pioneer, introducing streaming to the world. Suddenly, entertainment became accessible at the click of a button, leaving Blockbuster dazed and disoriented. However, the plot thickened. It was only when Netflix transitioned from DVDs to online streaming that it truly captured the mainstream audience. Still reaping substantial profits, Blockbuster watched as Netflix adopted a subscription-based model, revolutionizing how people consumed entertainment. This strategic pivot lured nonconsumers into Netflix's fold, prompting Blockbuster to respond with its own online services. By this time, however, Netflix had already surged onto an exponential trajectory, firmly establishing its presence in the market. Eventually, Blockbuster's inability to adapt to the rapidly changing landscape led to its demise. The Netflix versus Blockbuster saga shows the peril of overlooking disruptive innovations and, most importantly, the risks associated with the lack of Transformative Strategic Thinking

(TST) to challenge their own business model's assumptions in a dynamic world.

Key Takeaways

- Disruptive innovations are capable of transforming an industry or market by introducing a new product, service, technology, or business model that disrupts existing businesses.
- Disruptive innovations are processes that transform costly and complex offerings into more affordable and accessible alternatives.
- Disruptive innovations frequently originate from outsiders and entrepreneurial start-ups rather than well-established industry leaders.
- In the face of disruptive innovations, companies' incapability of challenging their business model assumptions may lead to competitiveness loss and, in the worst cases, to failure.

Understanding How Disruptive Innovation Affects Business Model Logics

As we mentioned earlier in this chapter, disruptive innovations wield the potential to reshape industries, forge new market leaders, and fundamentally alter the modus operandi of businesses. Throughout history, we have seen numerous examples of these innovations at play. Think about when personal computers burst onto the scene in the late 1970s and the 1980s. They played a big role in the decline of mainframe computers, making computing power accessible to individuals and small businesses. Another case in point is digital photography. It revolutionized how we capture, store, and share images, making film-based photography obsolete. And then there is the advent of smartphones—these compact devices that seamlessly blend calling, messaging, Internet use, and apps, causing a significant shift in communication and impacting multiple industries. Fast forward to today, we're witnessing the progression of a constellation of groundbreaking innovations such as artificial intelligence (AI) and machine learning, electric and self-driving vehicles, renewable energy solutions, and even technologies such as blockchains and crypto-currencies. These innovations have left many managers and entrepreneurs scratching their heads, wondering what comes next.

Nevertheless, history taught us that a salient trait among highly successful companies is their ability to embrace change and view disruptive innovations as opportunities rather than threats. A key principle of disruptive innovation theory is recognizing the need for new business models to thrive. Consider IBM as a prime example. They made a strategic shift from focusing solely on hardware, like mainframes, to becoming a provider of technology and services catering to businesses' evolving needs. In essence, the companies that flourish are the ones that see disruption as a chance to recalibrate their strategies and approaches. They understand that disruptive innovations can open doors to exciting new possibilities.

This ability to embrace change often comes from the creative thinking of entrepreneurs and managers, who are open to experimentation and questioning how things have always been done. This kind of mindset can lead to real transformations.

The TST toolkit that was introduced in the first part of this book (Chapters 1–5) can be used to train entrepreneurs and managers to think more creatively, especially when it comes to dealing with big changes and disruptive innovations. To this aim, the TST tool can be used in two main ways. First, it can be used to get a clearer picture of how our business model logic (BML) currently works (understanding the current assumptions) and how disruptive innovation affects it. Second, the TST tool can be employed to experiment with new ideas for transforming a BML, leveraging the new and potentially disruptive innovation (challenging the current assumptions).

Therefore, in a scenario of disruptive innovation, here's how to put the TST tool into action:

Step 1. Analyze the Current Business Model Logic

Use the TST framework to analyze your current BML. The analytical effort here is really important to gain a full understanding of the assumptions behind your business model. Go through each element of your BML—*meaning, experiential performance, resources, roles*, and *value equation*—by paying attention to all elements' subdimensions.

Step 2. Pinpoint the Vulnerable Element

Now, ask yourself, which elements of your BML might be most impacted by the disruptive innovation over time? And why?

The disruptive innovation might not be widespread yet, but it's crucial to envision how your BML could change when it does become mainstream. Your goal here is to pinpoint elements in your BML that could be vulnerable to the new technology's introduction.

Step 3. Experiment With a New Business Model Logic

Now, try to turn the threat into an opportunity. Focus on the element(s) you identified in the previous step. Experiment with different transformational practices to incorporate disruptive innovation into your BML. For instance, if you think the *meaning* of your offering is at risk, brainstorm ways to transform it on paper with a *shaping* practice. See how the other elements align when you make this change. Finally, you can reiterate the whole process, for example, transforming the experiential performance through a *stretching* practice. After adjusting the other elements, compare the new "shaping-driven" BML with the "stretching-driven" one to evaluate which has more potential. You can start the process with any of the five transformational practices illustrated in this book (Figure 6.1).

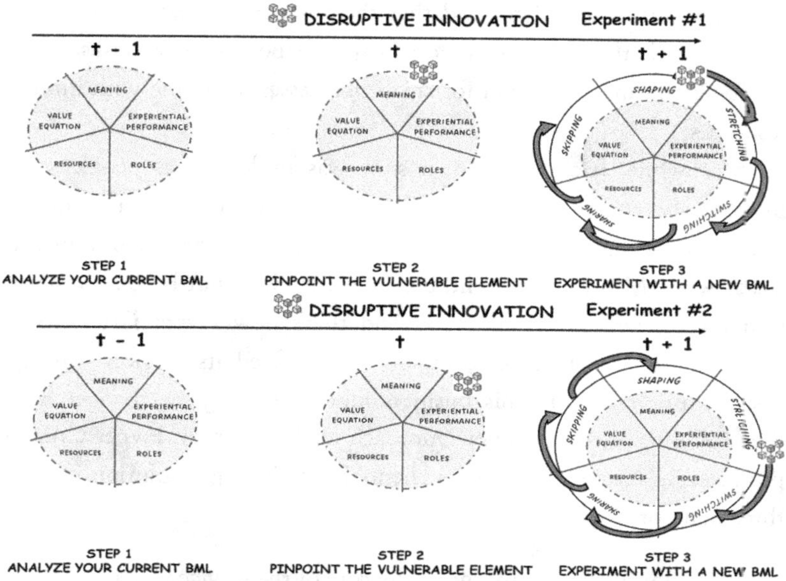

Figure 6.1 Using the TST tool to deal with disruptive innovation

Applying TST to Deal With Disruptive Innovation: The Case of Hyper Crunch

Hyper Crunch Before Being Disrupted

To better grasp the impact of adopting a TST approach in response to disruptive innovation, let's dive into the story of an entrepreneur who wasn't afraid to embrace change. When a disruptive innovation came knocking, he was well-prepared and ready to face it head-on. But let's start from the beginning.

Mehdi was an MBA student with a background in computer science when he decided to start his digital marketing business in 2018. His primary target was small businesses, such as local restaurants or grocery stores, seeking to build a presence online and grow their sales. Back then, if you were diving into digital marketing, you had two choices: freelancers or media agencies. But freelancers were hit or miss— sometimes you'd spend ages trying to find the right person, and even then, the results weren't always dependable. On the other hand, media agencies could be pretty pricey and surprise you with hidden clauses and extra costs. Mehdi realized that the absence of clear transparency, coupled with the challenge of quantifying labor-intensive tasks, often led to significant frustration for small businesses operating with limited resources.

Meanwhile, back in 2018, a shift was underway as people grew increasingly accustomed to subscription-based models for enjoying music, accessing workspaces, and consuming home entertainment. That's when Mehdi had a lightbulb moment: Why not have a subscription for marketing services, too? And that's how Hyper Crunch was born—a digital marketing company that offered its services through a subscription model. This business model was a game-changer back then, offering a fresh and new approach to the industry. Hyper Crunch promised to create value for its clients by designing a solution around three main principles:

1. Tailor-Made Approach: At the core of the service was a customized experience. The team of dedicated marketing specialists—the *crunchers*—would craft a unique digital strategy and create content precisely aligned with the client's objectives and preferences. This encompassed a range of activities, including activating free advertisements, crafting content, and posting on social media platforms.

2. Rapid Turnaround: Speed was a defining factor in the service. The entire process took less than three days, from the moment a client subscribed to the service to the delivery of a comprehensive digital strategy report and the content posting schedule across various social media channels. This swift turnaround ensured that clients could quickly start implementing their digital marketing initiatives.

3. Transparent and Clear Pricing: The service was designed with a straightforward pricing structure prioritizing transparency. Clients were offered a choice between three distinct monthly plans (Essential, Advanced, and Complete). Each plan came at an affordable price point, and they varied in the level of service

offered. This clear differentiation allowed customers to select the plan that best suited their needs and budget.

In brief, the service provided a custom approach to digital marketing, with dedicated teams tailoring strategies and content to individual client goals. The efficient delivery process ensured quick implementation, and the straightforward pricing options offered transparency and flexibility to cater to a range of client requirements.

The following figures show a more accurate description of the Hyper Crunch BML.

Hyper Crunch Meaning—Before Disruptive Innovation

Presented as a valuable solution for boosting sales, establishing a solid online presence, and reaching new markets, people love Hyper Crunch for offering an accessible yet dependable solution to externalize their marketing services without incurring unexpected costs (meaning end-use). Moreover, opting for a cost-effective subscription-based service can be particularly relevant during periods of staff downsizing, financial restructuring, or as an initial step toward exploring rebranding or strategic repositioning initiatives (meaning usage context). Finally, with its transparent pricing and the three-day delivery, Hyper Crunch becomes synonymous with trust, transparency, efficiency, achievement, accessibility, and stress alleviation (meaning symbolic significance). In essence, people love Hyper Crunch because it provides an *easily accessible and dependable means to achieve a complete online presence* (Figure 6.2).

Hyper Crunch Experiential Performance—Before Disruptive Innovation

The foundation of Hyper Crunch experiential performance rests on four core experiential building blocks (EBBs). The first one centers around providing a personalized digital strategy plan (EBB1) that is not only cost-effective but also transparent (EQ1), setting it apart from conventional media agencies, known for unexpected expenses and high fees (experiential benchmark 1—EBK1). Simultaneously, the

MEANING		
END-USE	**USAGE CONTEXT**	**SYMBOLIC SIGNIFICANCE**
For which purposes do people use the product/service?	In association with which other experiences the product/service is seen as relevant?	What feelings and emotions dose the product/service evoke?
Clients use Hyper Crunch for/when Clients use ...	Clients use Hyper Crunch in/with ...	Clients use Hyper Crunch to feel ...
they want to grow their sales they want to build a presence online	a rebranding strategy financial adjustments	trust transparency
they want to externalize their marketing activities they want to avoid unexpected costs	strategic repositioning staff restructuring	achievement efficiency
they want to reach new markets		accessibility stress relief

Figure 6.2 Hyper crunch meaning before disruptive innovation

Hyper Crunch service leverages a team of marketing experts to offer a swifter and more dependable solution (experiential quality 1-EQ1) compared to freelance options (EBK1). The second important aspect of the Hyper Crunch experiential performance pertains to the increase in online visibility (EBB2) that outperforms freelance approaches (EBK2) —by being more efficient and comprehensive (EQ2). This is achieved through robust advertising placement agreements and a diverse range of content offered by Hyper Crunch. Even when considering equivalent factors, Hyper Crunch remains notably more affordable (EQ2) than traditional agencies (EBK2). The third significant facet of the Hyper Crunch Experiential Performance revolves around enhanced community engagement (EBK3). This is facilitated by the service's capability to respond to reviews as part of the package, proving to be a more effective solution (EQ3) compared to freelancers (EBK3) and markedly more budget-friendly (EQ3) than conventional media agencies (EBK3). Finally, the inclusion of regular reporting and weekly meetings with the crunchers provides customers with the opportunity for continuous updates on their digital marketing performance (EBB4), instilling a heightened level of dependability (EQ4) compared to freelance options (EBK4) (Figure 6.3).

EXPERIENTIAL PERFORMANCE		
EXPERIENTIAL BUILDING BLOCKS (EBB)	**EXPERIENTIAL QUALITY (EQ)**	**EXPERIENTIAL BENCHMARK (EBK)**
What are the relevant aspects of the customer experience?	In which way do these aspects create more value?	Compared to what substitute/similar experiences?
With Hyper Crunch the user can	How?	Differently from ....
EBB.1 *OBTAIN A CUSTOM DIGITAL STRATEGY PLAN*	In a more AFFORDABLE way In a more TRANSPARENT way In a FASTER way In a more RELIABLE way	REGULAR MEDIA AGENCIES FREELANCERS
EBB.2 *INCREASE ONLINE VISIBILITY*	In a more EFFECTIVE way In a more COMPREHENSIVE way In a more AFFORDABLE way	FREELANCERS REGULAR MEDIA AGENCIES
EBB.3 *BE MORE ENGAGED WITH THE COMMUNITY*	In a more EFFECTIVE way In a more AFFORDABLE way	FREELANCERS

Figure 6.3 Hyper Crunch experiential performance before disruptive innovation

Hyper Crunch Resources—Before Disruptive Innovation

Content creators stand as a key resource within the Hyper Crunch BML. These individuals are responsible for executing a substantial portion of the customer's digital campaign. Notably, their proficiency lay not only in creativity but also in agility to meet the stringent demand for rapid delivery—an essential performance indicator for the service. Equally crucial are sales personnel who play a vital role in elucidating the value proposition of the service to customers. Additionally, the board of advisers holds paramount importance, as their endorsement plays a foundational role in establishing the company's credibility. Besides internal resources, external assets held substantial sway. Resources beyond the company's direct control, such as project management tools and partnerships with co-working spaces, incubators, and accelerators, play a pivotal role. These affiliations not only facilitate Hyper Crunch's growth but also provide tangible assets, networking opportunities, and strategic insights. Lastly, considering resources managed by customers themselves, case studies detailing the successes of companies utilizing Hyper Crunch are of utmost significance. These success stories contribute to the business model's credibility among prospects, while the clients' own networks act as a conduit for attracting new clientele through word-of-mouth referrals (Figure 6.4).

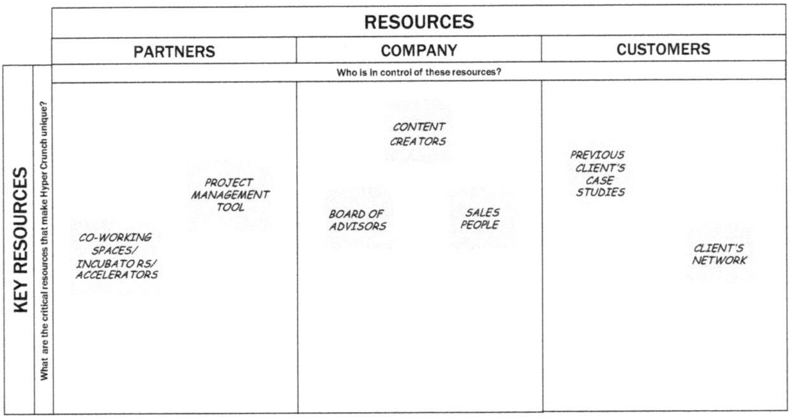

RESOURCES		
PARTNERS	COMPANY	CUSTOMERS
	Who is in control of these resources?	

Figure 6.4 Hyper Crunch resources before disruptive innovation

Hyper Crunch Roles—Before Disruptive Innovation

As for the onstage key activities, the customer's journey commences with a "discovery call" involving a Hyper Crunch team member. This interaction serves to grasp the campaign's objectives and budget. Upon mutual agreement, the customer proceeds to a demo call where the Hyper Crunch team presents their value proposition. Following this, the team dispatches an e-mail to the customer proposing the subscription plan. Once accepted, the customer begins the onboarding process by enrolling in the service online, providing requisite information, and completing payments. Customers can also activate add-ons, such as articles or position papers, if they require supplementary materials beyond the plan. As the onboarding procedure begins, the customer is responsible for validating marketing content and participating in weekly meetings with the Hyper Crunch team. These meetings serve as a platform for receiving updates and engaging in discussions. Moreover, the Hyper Crunch team provides periodic reports containing campaign performance statistics. At the backstage level, Hyper Crunch undertakes a range of tasks. This includes formulating a personalized campaign strategy, generating content, managing the client community, devising a content delivery schedule, facilitating customer image rebranding, monitoring the campaign, implementing adjustments, and optimizing performance. In the realm of support activities, the company

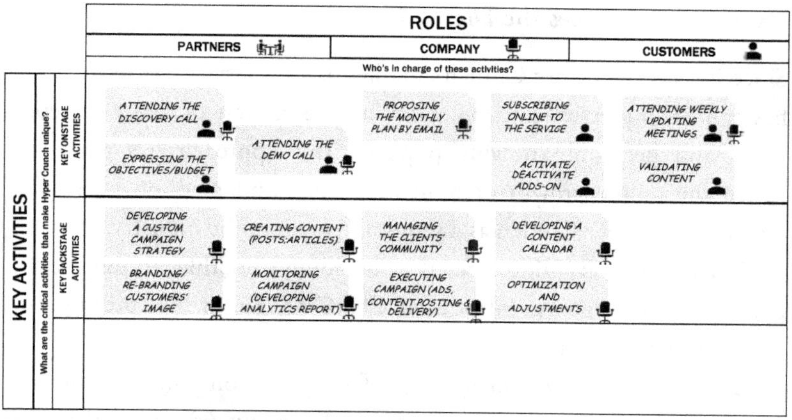

			ROLES		
		PARTNERS 🧑‍🤝‍🧑	**COMPANY** 👤		**CUSTOMERS** 👤
			Who's in charge of these activities?		

KEY ACTIVITIES
What are the critical activities that make Hyper Crunch unique?

KEY ONSTAGE ACTIVITIES

ATTENDING THE DISCOVERY CALL 👤🧑	ATTENDING THE DEMO CALL 👤🧑	PROPOSING THE MONTHLY PLAN BY EMAIL 👤	SUBSCRIBING ONLINE TO THE SERVICE 👤	ATTENDING WEEKLY UPDATING MEETINGS 👤🧑
EXPRESSING THE OBJECTIVES/BUDGET 👤			ACTIVATE/ DEACTIVATE ADDS-ON 👤	VALIDATING CONTENT 👤

KEY BACKSTAGE ACTIVITIES

DEVELOPING A CUSTOM CAMPAIGN STRATEGY 👤	CREATING CONTENT (POSTS;ARTICLES) 🧑	MANAGING THE CLIENTS' COMMUNITY 👤	DEVELOPING A CONTENT CALENDAR 👤
BRANDING/ RE-BRANDING CUSTOMERS' IMAGE 👤	MONITORING CAMPAIGN (DEVELOPING ANALYTICS REPORT) 🧑	EXECUTING CAMPAIGN (ADS, CONTENT POSTING & DELIVERY) 👤	OPTIMIZATION AND ADJUSTMENTS 👤

Figure 6.5 Hyper Crunch roles before disruptive innovation

establishes placement agreements and designs an onboarding ques-ion-naire. Meanwhile, a partnered entity shoulders the responsibility of developing and maintaining the platform (Figure 6.5).

Hyper Crunch Value Equation—Before Disruptive Innovation

The value equation's primary benefits for the customer center around transparency in offerings and pricing. These include a streamlined customer journey, eliminating unnecessary touchpoints, and facilitating an uncomplicated, automated onboarding process. This is coupled with a top-tier digital marketing strategy characterized by its quality yet affordability and expedited delivery. The affordability of the subscription-based model promotes broader accessibility of marketing services, which is particularly beneficial for small businesses facing resource constraints. Moreover, customers enjoy having a dedicated specialist at their disposal, ensuring regular updates and discussions about adjustments and the option for a tailored rebranding strategy when necessary. Regarding the efforts required from customers, they entail committing to a minimum 3-month subscription. Customers are also tasked with articulating their campaign needs clearly, engaging in the onboarding procedure, responding to the questionnaire, and actively participating in weekly meetings to assess campaign performance and validate content (Figure 6.6).

Hyper Crunch Faces the Disruption

Since its launch, Hyper Crunch's marketing-as-a-service platform model has gained impressive traction, catching the interest of many entrepreneurs and becoming notably popular. This approach has effectively fueled the online growth of numerous small and medium businesses, establishing Hyper Crunch as a standout player in the industry.

But just as everything seemed to be going smoothly, an unexpected twist emerged: OpenAI introduced ChatGPT, a tool that promised to change things forever.

The term *artificial intelligence*, referring to computers mimicking human understanding, has been around for about 60 years. Throughout its history, AI has alternated breakthroughs, setbacks, and times of renewed interest. Coined in the 1950s by John McCarthy, AI gained momentum in the 1960s through workshops and expert systems. The 1970s emphasized symbolic AI and rule-based systems, while the 1980s faced challenges during the *AI winter* due to inflated expectations. In the 2000s, thanks to the availability of large datasets and more sophisticated algorithms, machine-learning techniques improved till the 2010s, marked by deep learning in speech and language. Then, AI became integrated across industries, continuing into the 2020s with reinforcement learning, generative models, and, of course, ethical questions. Initially, AI found applications across various domains, such as chatbots and language translation, image recognition for autonomous vehicles and diagnostics, machine learning for predictions and recommendations, robotics for manufacturing, and AI-driven optimization for decision making. However, for most of its history, AI remained a prerogative of computer scientists or tech-savvies who would embed it (among many other things) in product applications to create delightful customer experiences, such as Netflix's personalized suggestions or those fun Instagram filters that give you puppy ears and more. But when ChatGPT came out in November 2022, everything suddenly changed.

Suddenly, regular folks who aren't tech wizards could tap into the AI's potential, helping out with writing, translating, or coding, sparking a mix of awe and concern about where we fit in the future.

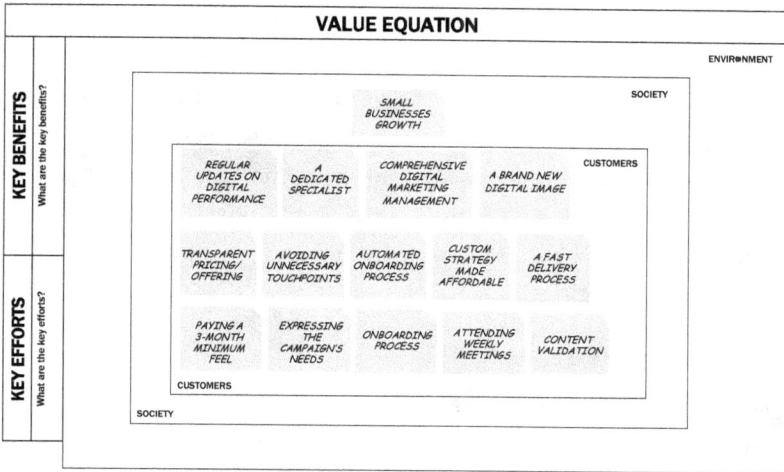

VALUE EQUATION

| | | ENVIRONMENT |
| | | SOCIETY |

KEY BENEFITS — *What are the key benefits?*

KEY EFFORTS — *What are the key efforts?*

SMALL BUSINESSES GROWTH

CUSTOMERS

| REGULAR UPDATES ON DIGITAL PERFORMANCE | A DEDICATED SPECIALIST | COMPREHENSIVE DIGITAL MARKETING MANAGEMENT | A BRAND NEW DIGITAL IMAGE |

| TRANSPARENT PRICING/ OFFERING | AVOIDING UNNECESSARY TOUCHPOINTS | AUTOMATED ONBOARDING PROCESS | CUSTOM STRATEGY MADE AFFORDABLE | A FAST DELIVERY PROCESS |

| PAYING A 3-MONTH MINIMUM FEEL | EXPRESSING THE CAMPAIGN'S NEEDS | ONBOARDING PROCESS | ATTENDING WEEKLY MEETINGS | CONTENT VALIDATION |

CUSTOMERS

SOCIETY

Figure 6.6 Hyper Crunch value equation before disruptive innovation

But let's go back to Mehdi's story. As a computer scientist and tech enthusiast, Mehdi had already dabbled with AI tools driven by curiosity well before the advent of ChatGPT. He had found those tools somewhat clunky and underwhelming, so there wasn't much cause for concern initially. Even when the ChatGPT 3.0 was launched, his reaction was more like: "Interesting, not quite there yet, but interesting!" With that thought in mind, he headed off for his Christmas break without much worry. However, upon returning to his office and trying out the new ChatGPT 3.5, his reaction shifted to a resounding "wow," and genuine concern began to set in. After initially brushing it aside for a couple of weeks, Mehdi gradually started recognizing the growing impact of AI. The first two weeks of January saw a constant stream of business and tech news reporting on companies launching their own AI-powered tools and platforms. The signs of disruption were unmistakable. At this point, he gathered his team and told them, "We need to take action, or we're going to be disrupted."

Indeed, the rise of AI-powered tools such as ChatGPT presents a substantial challenge to the digital marketing landscape, particularly in content creation. These tools wield remarkable ability in crafting flawless, on-demand content, including captions, social media posts, articles, newsletters, and more. Consequently, the reliance on agencies for services such as copywriting or routine tasks could wane. This shift raises the possibility of reduced demand for digital marketing agencies as businesses turn to AI for content creation. Fueled by this perspective, Mehdi took a deep breath, rolled up his sleeves, and embraced the inevitable transformation, drawing from his tech background. He embarked on developing a tool that was about to transform the assumptions behind his business model forever.

Hyper Crunch After the Disruption

Once the ChatGPT tool was introduced, it became evident that the traditional role of marketing-as-a-service companies in content creation could be readily substituted by AI tools by their previous customers. This realization prompted Mehdi to initiate a business model transformation, commencing with this inevitable shift: switching with customers his company's traditional role in content creation.

In Chapter 4, where we delve into how to initiate a BML logic transformation by *switching* the *roles* (the fourth element of the BML) you might recall that switching the roles brings about consequences not only in terms of substituting the actors overseeing a specific activity (referred to as *Switching by Changing the Key Actors*) but also in reshaping the flow of the key activities (referred to as *Switching by Changing the Flow of Activities*). This means that by entrusting the key activity of content creation to customers, you are not solely changing the key actor responsible for this crucial task, but you're also changing the flow of this activity from backstage to onstage. Consequently, shifting a key activity from being backstage (not visible to the customer) to onstage (visible to the customer) opens up opportunities to enhance customer experience.

And that's exactly what Mehdi did: He conceived a solution that enabled enterprises to harness the capabilities of AI for autonomously executing their digital marketing tasks more efficiently. Drawing from his extensive experience in digital marketing and his education as a computer scientist, he leveraged the disruptive innovation that was about to disrupt his original business model and channeled it into creating a support tool for companies in their transitional journey: Hyper Crunch AI.

Hyper Crunch AI is a platform tool accessible to companies of all scales, empowering them to automatically generate their weekly marketing content within a mere five-minute span. The central objective of Hyper Crunch AI revolves around empowering content creators with AI-driven tools, facilitating the creation of high-quality content at an accelerated pace while bolstering efficiency. This is achieved by providing a platform that harmonizes creativity and technology. Here, AI serves to streamline content creation and enhance the distinct brand image of each customer, ultimately boosting productivity and forging a path for innovating their marketing content and storytelling. But, let's go in order.

By employing the TST tool to analyze this case study, we can observe that Mehdi initiates his BML transformation through a *switching* practice. He strategically transferred one of the key activities— "creating content"—previously executed by his company in the old business model, directly to the customer. As a result, this activity shifted from being a backstage activity to an onstage one (Figure 6.7).

Starting from this simple *switching* maneuver, a whole redefinition of the *Roles* unfolds in the Hyper Crunch BML. This encompasses introducing new key activities, redistributing responsibilities among the company, customers, and partners, and establishing a completely new flow of activities.

Hyper Crunch Roles—After Disruptive Innovation

Within the new BML, the customer embarks on a journey where they need to enroll and subscribe to the service (at a base rate of 69€ per month). This process entails incorporating their company's website link onto the platform, which then generates tailor-made content and content guidelines within five minutes. These generated materials align with the brand's identity and are tailored to the company's writing style. The customer is also tasked with integrating the platform with their company's social media channels and mailing list, promptly posting the content, and dispatching newsletters.

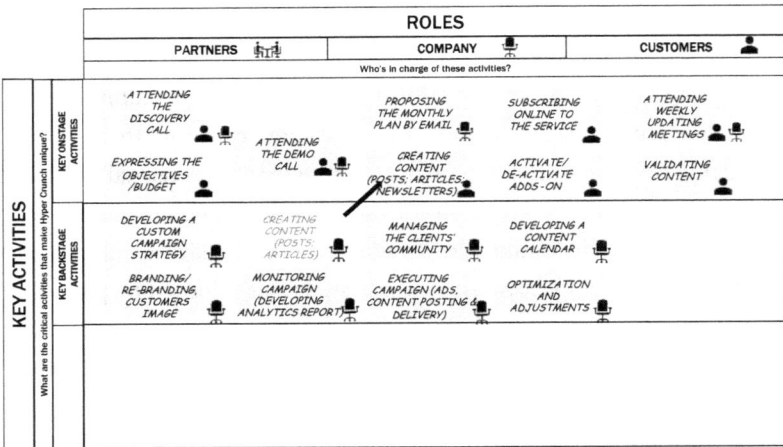

Figure 6.7 Hyper Crunch—BML transformation by switching the roles

A substantial portion of the tasks, once performed behind the scenes by Hyper Crunch, now transition to the customer's realm (onstage).

Conversely, the company (Hyper Crunch AI) assumes responsibility for guaranteeing the smooth execution of operations, ensuring a consistent flow of personalized content. They also extend support through aiding platform usage, facilitated by a designated account success manager for premium users. Moreover, they engage in custom AI model training for premium users. In this new BML, new support activities encompass the creation of an extensive library housing 12,000 content pieces to stimulate novel creative endeavors (Figure 6.8).

Hyper Crunch Experiential Performance—After Disruptive Innovation

To realign the BML to the new roles, the new experiential performance is now built upon novel EBBs. These encompass innovative features such as the empowerment to "design their own digital marketing campaign." Through the newly developed platform, Hyper Crunch AI users can autonomously construct a comprehensive digital marketing campaign from inception to completion. This process is facilitated by inputting essential details, including their website URL, preferred

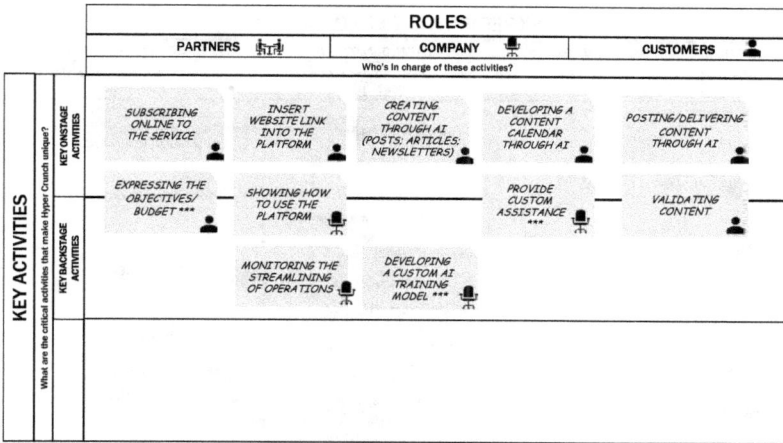

		ROLES		
		PARTNERS	COMPANY	CUSTOMERS
			Who's in charge of these activities?	

Figure 6.8 Hyper Crunch roles after disruptive innovation

content type (articles, social media posts, emails, etc.), and integrating their social media platforms and mailing lists. Moreover, thanks to the AI builder, the integrated platform gives users complete command over their campaigns. This sophisticated tool not only generates weekly content seamlessly but also orchestrates direct scheduling onto their channels. This ensures the consistent and vibrant maintenance of their social media presence. Notably, what sets Hyper Crunch AI apart from other freely accessible AI tools is the exclusive provision of customized AI model training, a premium feature (Figure 6.9).

Hyper Crunch Resources—After Disruptive Innovation

Consequently, a shift in the resource regime will follow due to the realignment. Resources that were once indispensable, like content creators, will no longer be needed. At the same time, the AI builder and its algorithms will emerge as pivotal for the business model's success. Notably, customers' existing marketing assets, including their websites, will take on an essential role as input data for generating aligned content. Concurrently, the repository of content pieces within the library will play a crucial role in stimulating the creation of innovative and novel materials (Figure 6.10).

EXPERIENTIAL PERFORMANCE		
EXPERIENTIAL BUILDING BLOCKS (EBB)	EXPERIENTIAL QUALITY (EQ)	EXPERIENTIAL BENCHMARK (EBK)
What are the relevant aspects of the customer experience?	In which way do these aspects create more value?	Compared to what substitute/similar experiences?
With **Hyper Crunch** the user can	How?	Differently from ....
EBB.1 OBTAIN A CUSTOM DIGITAL STRATEGY PLAN	In a more AFFORDABLE way / In a more EFFICIENT way / In a more AUTOMATED way / In a more RELIABLE way	REGULAR MEDIA AGENCIES / FREELANCERS
EBB.2 INCREASE ONLINE VISIBILITY	In a more EFFECTIVE way / In a more AFFORDABLE way / In a more COMPREHENSIVE way	FREELANCERS
EBB.3 DESIGN THEIR DIGITAL MARKETING CAMPAIGN	In a more INDEPENDENT way / In a more AFFORDABLE way / In an EASIER way	FREELANCERS / REGULAR MEDIA AGENCIES / FREE AI TOOLS
EBB.4 FULLY CONTROL THEIR OWN DIGITAL MARKETING CAMPAIGN	In a more INDEPENDENT way / In an EASIER way	FREELANCERS / REGULAR MEDIA AGENCIES
EBB.5 OBTAIN AI MODEL TRAINING	In a MORE CUSTOM way	FREE AI TOOLS

Figure 6.9 Hyper Crunch experiential performance after disruptive innovation

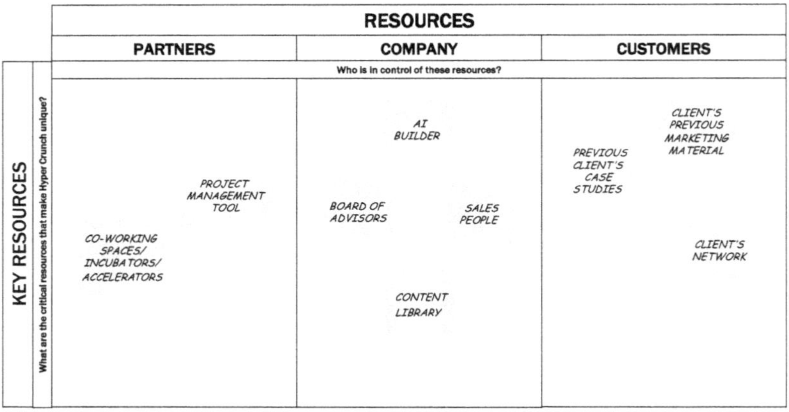

Figure 6.10 Hyper Crunch resources after disruptive innovation

Hyper Crunch Value Equation—After Disruptive Innovation

Given the new configuration of the BML, the value equation will transform, yielding new advantages for customers. These encompass automated content creation and delivery, the potential for substantial reductions in marketing expenditures, and the ability to save time allocated for marketing tasks. Conversely, the revised value equation introduces new efforts associated with furnishing input data for the AI builder and overseeing the delivery schedule, which now operates without intermediaries. Nevertheless, these tasks entail minimal effort intensity, as the platform renders these operations predominantly automatic, necessitating only mere supervision. The platform's predominantly automatic operations, requiring only occasional supervision, ensure that clients can contribute to the marketing process without significant time or energy investments. Moreover, the platform extends a comprehensive productivity suite, equipping customers with tools to manage various aspects, including video calls and emails. This not only enhances operational efficiency but also supports remote collaboration, reducing the need for physical travel and its associated environmental impact (Figure 6.11).

Hyper Crunch Meaning—After Disruptive Innovation

Ultimately, this transformation's new meaning rests upon new end-uses centered around optimizing users' harnessing of AI and streamlining marketing tasks through an AI builder. This empowering tool enables them to entrust their content creation to automation, virtually freeing them from constant attention. Within the new meaning's usage context, the narrative extends to encompass the customer's journey toward seamless AI integration into their operations. The new meaning's symbolic significance is enriched with a sense of velocity derived from the capability to generate marketing content in the blink of an eye. It also gives a feeling of empowerment through the platform's capacity for complete control over marketing activities using the AI builder. Consequently, the newfound reason why people love Hyper Crunch AI crystallizes into this: "*It's like having an adept marketing specialist at one's beck and call, 24/7*" (Figure 6.12).

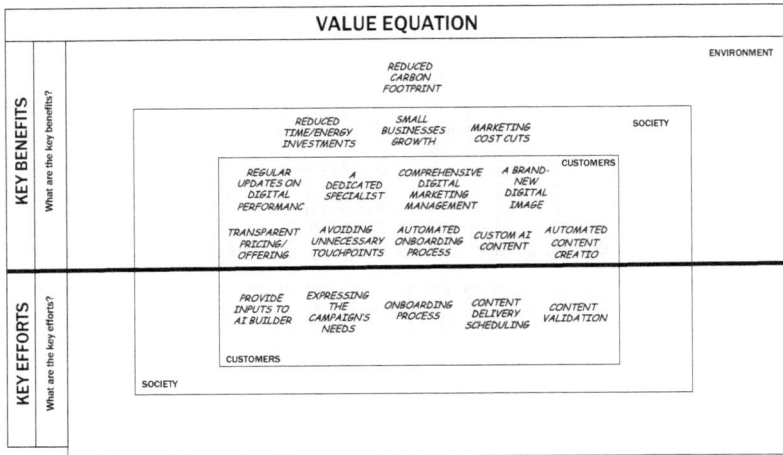

Figure 6.11 Hyper Crunch value equation after disruptive innovation

MEANING		
END-USE	**USAGE CONTEXT**	**SYMBOLIC SIGNIFICANCE**
For which purposes do people use the product/service?	In association with which other experiences the product/service is seen as relevant?	What feelings and emotions does the product/service evoke?
Clients use Hyper Crunch for/when ...	Clients use Hyper Crunch in/with ...	Clients use Hyper Crunch to feel ...
they want to grow their sales they want to build a presence online	integration of AI in their operations financial adjustments	empowered transparency
they want to automate their marketing activities they want to avoid unexpected costs	strategic repositioning staff restructuring	achievement efficiency
they want to reach new markets they aim to optimize their utilization		velocity stress relief

Figure 6.12 Hyper Crunch meaning after disruptive innovation

So What?

The tale of Hyper Crunch shows the potential of adopting the right mindset to tackle tough times and emerge from them even stronger. Mehdi's journey illustrates the power of embracing change rather than resisting it. When AI came knocking and threatened to disrupt his business, Mehdi undertook a comprehensive assessment of his current BML. He realized that some of his old assumptions, specifically those tied to the BML roles, were no longer tenable due to disruptive technology. So, he didn't sit back. He pinpointed the vulnerable element within his structure (the company's key role in content creation) and initiated the transformation from there (BML transformation by switching the roles). This is what we mean by adopting TST and what we aim to help you develop through the methods in this book. By the time we write, Hyper Crunch AI has just been launched. It's too soon to say if it'll outperform the old business model, but here's the bottom line: Mehdi is out there experimenting. He's making adjustments, gaining new clients, learning from them, and making mistakes—all of which epitomize the essence of TST.

Mehdi's story underscores the significance of approaching disruptive innovations with a TST mindset for strategically navigating uncertain times and using them to foster innovation and growth.

Chapter Overview

In this chapter, we illustrate the first of the three managerial challenges likely to affect companies' current logic of value creation: *disruptive innovation*. Disruptive innovations displace established technologies throughout a long-term process that gradually sees their introduction in the niche markets to reach the mainstream market. This can reshape industries in the long run. Failing to adapt business models in response to disruptive innovation can result in loss of competitiveness or even failure. Successful companies historically thrive by embracing change and perceiving disruptive innovation as opportunities by transforming their BML. This adaptability often stems from creative thinking among entrepreneurs and managers, characterized by openness to experimentation and questioning current assumptions. The TST tool can be helpful in cultivating this mindset by training entrepreneurs and managers to manage substantial changes and disruptive innovation creatively. It serves two main purposes: First, understanding the current business assumptions and their interaction with disruptive innovation, and second, experimenting with new transformative ideas using the innovation to challenge existing assumptions. The chapter concludes by analyzing the case of Hyper Crunch, emphasizing the strategic importance of adopting a TST approach to navigate uncertainty presented by disruptive innovations.

CHAPTER 7

Black Swan Events

What Will You Learn in This Chapter?

You will:

- Understand which aspects define a black swan event.
- Learn how black swan events can affect a Business Model Logic (BML).
- Understand how to deal with a black swan event by using the TST tool.
- Understand the implications of adopting a TST in the face of a black swan event from a real-world business case.

Challenge #2 Black Swan Events: Decoding the Unexpected

Long before the world discovered the vastness of Australia, a prevailing belief held the Old World in its grip—a belief so strong it seemed unchallengeable. The conviction was simple: all swans were white. This idea was considered an undeniable truth, supported by generations of evidence, until 1967. That year, Dutch explorer Willem de Vlamingh journeyed to Australia and encountered a remarkable bird, scientifically known as *Cygnus atratus*. Its shining black plumage astonished the ornithologists. The discovery of the black swan became more than a zoological finding; it turned into a powerful metaphor highlighting a key limitation in our understanding. It shows how fragile our knowledge can be, as a single observation can challenge a broad belief built on centuries of sighting only white swans.

Nassim Taleb, a Lebanese-American philosopher, a mathematician, and an expert in financial mathematics, later built upon this ornithological metaphor. In his acclaimed 2007 book, *The Black Swan: The Impact of the Highly Impossible,* Taleb introduced his audience to his theory of black swan events—a view that challenges conventional wisdom and highlights the extraordinary impact of highly improbable events.

A black swan event has three main defining attributes:

1. Unpredictability: It is an unforeseeable outlier, so unprecedented that no prior events could hint at its possibility.
2. Extreme impact: It has an extraordinary impact with severe and widespread consequences.
3. Hindsight illumination: Only after the event occurs can we explain it, making us believe we should have seen it coming.

To explore a concrete example, let's go back to September 25, 2008, when Lehman Brothers, the fourth-largest investment bank in the United States, declared bankruptcy. As many would recall, the event triggered an immediate crash in the stock market, with the Dow Jones, the main index of the New York Stock Exchange, plummeting by over 504 points (the highest loss since 9/11). Lehman Brothers had long exceeded the exposure limit to mortgages granted to families encouraged by the growth of the real estate market. However, it was mistakenly deemed "too big to fail," and its bankruptcy caught many off guard. The repercussions were cast and far-reaching. The interconnectedness of financial institutions set off a chain reaction of failures and bailouts, exposing how tightly integrated the global financial system had become. This led to a severe global recession, massive job losses, and a sharp decline in economic activity. Housing markets collapsed, major financial institutions faced insolvency, and credit markets froze. The crisis left enduring impacts on economies worldwide.

In the aftermath of that fateful day, experts and analysts were left scratching their heads. How could this have happened? How had they missed the signs? The crisis laid bare the fragility of a system many had taken for granted. In the years leading up to the crisis, the global economy thrived, markets soared, and confidence was high. Yet beneath the surface, the intricate web of financial instruments grew more complex, with mortgages bundled and sold like never before. Hindsight illuminated the cracks in the system. Systemic vulnerabilities, such as the proliferation of complex financial instruments (like mortgage-backed securities—MBS—and collateralized debt obligations), once heralded as innovations and inadequate regulatory oversight, were now seen as ticking time bombs.

Many companies had more trouble obtaining credit for operations, expansion, and investment during the crisis. Simultaneously, a decline in consumer spending prompted numerous companies to rethink their business models. For instance, in 2009, General Motors (GM), one of the world's largest car and truck manufacturers, filed for Chapter 11 bankruptcy protection. The U.S. government extended GM's financial assistance through loans and equity stakes to prevent its collapse. This intervention came with conditions, including the mandate for GM to undergo a significant restructuring, emphasizing operational efficiency and innovation in its product offerings. This led GM to accelerate its efforts toward more sustainable and fuel-efficient vehicles. An example of this effort was the Chevrolet Volt. Also known as the iCar, it represented a pivotal moment in GM's design philosophy, as it stood as the first-ever series plug-in hybrid concept car presented by a major car manufacturer.

In summary, the 2007 financial crisis is a clear example of a black swan event. It was unexpected, had a major impact on the global economy, and was only fully understood afterward as experts analyzed the contributing factors. The case of GM illustrates how black swan events can profoundly affect business models, with both positive and negative consequences. As Nassim Taleb suggests, instead of trying to predict future black swans, we should focus on accepting their inevitability and being prepared to respond to whatever happens.

Key Takeaways

- Black swan events are unforeseeable outliers that are so unprecedented that no prior events or models can hint at their possibility.
- Black swan events have an extraordinary impact and massive consequences, often altering the course of history in significant ways.
- Only after a black swan event has occurred can we explain its existence, leading us to believe that we should have seen it coming.
- We shouldn't focus on predicting future black swan events but on acknowledging their inevitability and ensuring preparedness to respond to them.
- Embracing adaptability in response to black swan events can help companies reevaluate their business model assumptions and improve their competitiveness.

Understanding How Black Swan Events Affect Business Model Logics

As mentioned earlier, black swan events are unpredictable, high-impact occurrences that often seem obvious in hindsight. Examples range from historic events such as World War I and the 9/11 attacks to financial shocks such as Black Monday and natural disasters such as the Indian Ocean earthquake and tsunami in 2004.

While black swan events are often associated with adversity, their impact can be positive or negative, depending on how individuals or companies respond to uncertainty. The GM example we discussed earlier shows how unexpected events can lead to innovation. However, not every company has the luxury of a government intervention to ensure survival. Therefore, for most businesses, navigating black swan events often hinges on their adaptability and willingness to embrace change, question their assumptions, and explore alternative business models.

Consider the recent COVID-19 pandemic. It's a classic example of a black swan event, catching us all off guard with its global reach and unforeseen complexity. Remember how our routines changed? People went from hitting up concerts and clubs every week to bingeing on Netflix shows and having virtual happy hours on Zoom. And who could forget the sudden craze for home baking that caused a crazy rush on flour in supermarkets?

All these lifestyle changes posed serious challenges to industries such as live entertainment, travel, education, and sports. Yet, amid this chaos, some companies managed not only to weather the storm but also to find new opportunities in it. For example, many gyms quickly transitioned to offering online workout classes and training sessions by developing or expanding their own digital fitness platforms. Some restaurants quickly pivoted to emphasize takeout and delivery options, enhanced their online ordering systems, and implemented contactless payment options to minimize physical contact between staff and customers. Some even designed and offered meal kits, allowing customers to recreate their favorite dishes at home. Hospitality companies like Airbnb adapted by promoting longer term stays and local travel experiences, capturing a market of remote workers seeking more extended accommodations. For some of these companies, these shifts in the business model stayed after the pandemic, resulting in a gain in performance and innovation, allowing them to better compete even in the post-COVID era.

In the context of black swan events, the TST tool can be used in both scrutinizing the existing BML for potential vulnerabilities and exploring alternative logic for business model transformations. Specifically, when facing a black swan event, using the TST tool involves a simple three-step process (Figure 7.1).

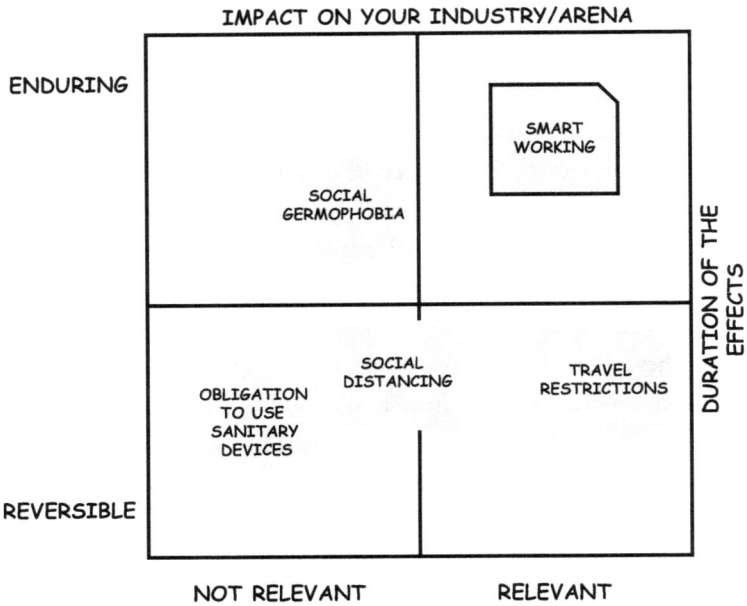

Figure 7.1 *Understand the black swan event's impact—Ex. Covid-19/ Airbnb*

Step 1 . Understanding the Impact of the Black Swan Event

A black swan event has the power to swiftly alter the landscape of an industry or arena, given its unforeseen and extreme nature. Take a moment to think about the significant shifts that may affect the sphere in which your business operates. Consider the black swan event's primary social, economic, and political repercussions. Do you anticipate these shifts to be enduring or potentially reversible? Focus on the changes that are relevant to your industry and are likely to have lasting effects. Refer to the example represented in Figure 7.1 for guidance on conducting this assessment.

Step 2. Analyze the Business Model Logic and Identify Vulnerable Element(s)

For the second step, use the TST framework to analyze your existing business model logic (BML). This is important for understanding the assumptions behind your business model. Review each part of your

BML—meaning, experiential performance (EP), resources, roles, and value equation—and consider their sub-dimensions. Then ask: which parts of your BML are most likely to be affected by the identified black swan event? The goal is to find out which elements of your BML might be impacted by the black swan event.

Step 3. Experiment With a New Business Model Logic

Direct attention to the element(s) you pinpointed in the previous step. Engage in experimental exercises, starting each transformation from the identified "fragile" element(s). Employ the corresponding transformational practice (i.e., *shaping, stretching, sharing, switching, and swapping*). The goal is to generate distinct iterations of new BMLs on paper, providing a basis for comparison and further experimentation as you craft your future business model (Figure 7.2).

Applying TST to Deal With Black Swan Events Technology: The Case of MoreNFT

MoreNFT Before the Black Swan

To show how Transformative Strategic Thinking (TST) can help handle black swan events, let's follow the journey of three young entrepreneurs venturing into the NFT (Non-Fungible Tokens) industry. After months of hard work on their brainchild, when they thought they were on the brink of something big, the NFT market takes a wild turn. Suddenly, they're back to the drawing board, reimagining their whole BML. But let's proceed with order. NFTs are digital certificates of ownership or authenticity, using blockchain technology. Unlike cryptocurrencies, NFTs are unique and cannot be exchanged one-to-one. They are used for digital art, collectibles, virtual real estate, and in-game items, proving the uniqueness and ownership of digital or physical items with a digital counterpart.

The NFT scene exploded during the 2020–2021 cryptocurrency bull market, providing plenty of investment opportunities. With COVID-19 keeping everyone at home, the Internet became the go-to

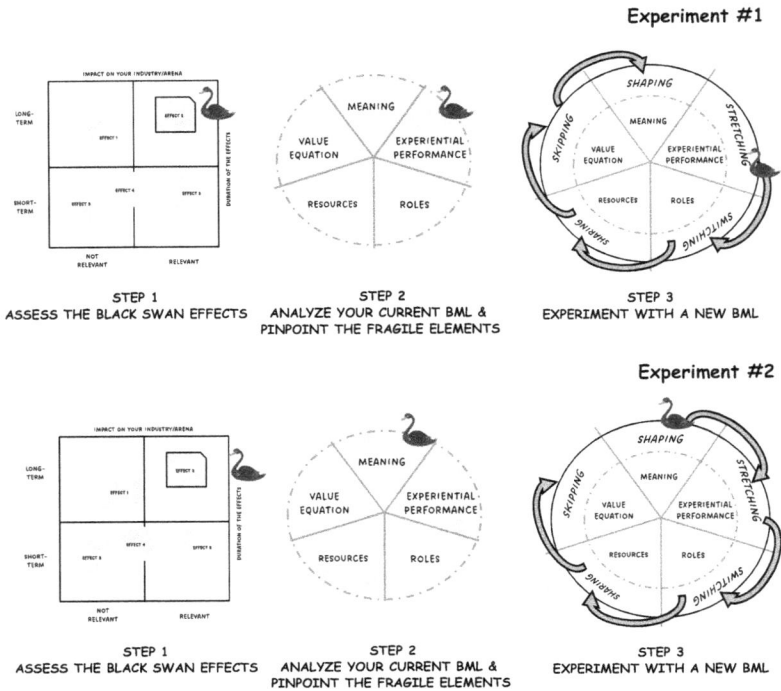

Figure 7.2 *Using the TST tool to deal with black swan events*

for fun and entertainment (remember the Travis Scott concert in the metaverse?). As physical art galleries and events faced closures or restrictions, artists and collectors shifted toward the digital sphere. Economic uncertainty during the pandemic led people to explore alternative investments, boosting the NFT market. By 2021, NFTs gained popularity with endorsements from celebrities like Tom Brady, Kim Kardashian, and Snoop Dogg. Luxury fashion brands entered the NFT space, selling exclusive collections to boost their image and profit. Early NFT projects made huge profits, leading many to seek ways to profit from NFT art or find the best NFTs to invest in.

Seeing the potential, our trio of entrepreneurs started to work on developing MoreNFT, a pioneering NFT marketplace that empowers creators and streamlines the NFT collection launch process. They identified a crucial gap in the market—most major NFT platforms, like Opensea, were primarily oriented toward the secondary market, where existing NFTs were bought and sold. There was less emphasis on the primary market, where a buyer directly purchases an NFT (minted) from its original creator. This meant that creators who wished to release their own NFT collections had to build their landing page or create one NFT at a time under the terms and conditions of the platform. This process demanded a certain level of expertise in the field and implied navigating complex procedures.

To address this, MoreNFT was conceived as a platform empowering creators to easily and collaboratively develop their projects, unlocking the full potential of NFTs. This not only provided investment opportunities but also extended services to a diverse community of creators, including brands and celebrities. To set itself apart, MoreNFT would have introduced its own governance token - the MRN - offering additional benefits to users. This innovative business model centered around three key elements:

1. The Factory: Exclusive projects and collections crafted by content creators, brands, and celebrities, all rigorously validated by their project recruiting team.
2. The Marketplace: Enabling users to buy and sell NFTs on Ethereum and Polygon blockchains, with rewards in MRN and WETH (Wrapped Ether—a tokenized version of ETH, the Ethereum cryptocurrency).
3. The Community: Through a decentralized autonomous organization (DAO), users actively participate in decision-making processes, shaping the destiny of tokens allocated for developing and growing the entire MoreNFT ecosystem.

The following section illustrates a more accurate MoreNFT BML description.

MoreNFT Meaning—Before Black Swan

Thanks to its dual focus on the primary and secondary markets and its unique factory model dedicated to nurturing artists and brands, people would love MoreNFT not only for its investment potential and NFT collection opportunities but also for the invaluable support and visibility it offers, particularly for newcomers (*meaning end-use*).

Moreover, this emphasis on building a community of artists, celebrities, and brands allows for seamless integration of the NFT experience with buyers' interests in music, fashion, gaming, art, and entertainment, fostering vibrant engagement within these communities. For creators, building a collection can strategically expand their reach to diverse customer bases. Meanwhile, the marketplace provides traders and speculative investors opportunities to diversify their portfolios (meaning usage context). Finally, while MoreNFT serves experienced users, it is specifically designed with early users, especially creators, in mind. Through reward systems for loyal users who choose to resell their minted NFTs on the same platform, as well as marketing and promotional support for emerging creators, and the establishment of a DAO with an associated governance token, MoreNFT empowers its users and involves them in important decisions regarding the platform. This inclusive approach makes users (creators, collectors, and traders) feel supported, smart, and in step with the times regarding their investment choices (meaning symbolic significance).

Ultimately, people would love MoreNFT because it would let them feel part of a digital family that guides them into the world of NFTs (Figure 7.3).

MoreNFT Experiential Performance—Before Black Swan

The foundation of MoreNFT EP rests on four core EBBs. The first one centers around facilitating NFT transactions (EBB1). MoreNFT outperforms tokenless NFT marketplaces (EBK1) like OpenSea by introducing its own token, MRN. This allows users to buy and sell NFTs on Ethereum and Polygon blockchains while enjoying additional benefits. MRN stakers receive a commission from sales conducted in WETH, and engaging in trading or staking activities further accumulates MRN rewards.

To combat inflation, 5 percent of each NFT sale's value is burned, reducing the total MRN supply. MRN also serves as a governance token for DAO initiatives. This results in a more rewarding and empowering

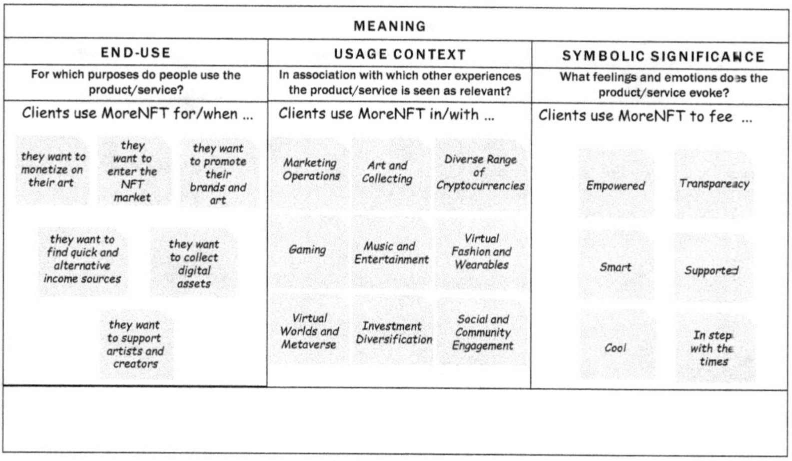

MEANING								
END-USE			USAGE CONTEXT			SYMBOLIC SIGNIFICANCE		
For which purposes do people use the product/service?			In association with which other experiences the product/service is seen as relevant?			What feelings and emotions does the product/service evoke?		
Clients use MoreNFT for/when ...			Clients use MoreNFT in/with ...			Clients use MoreNFT to fee ...		
they want to monetize on their art	they want to enter the NFT market	they want to promote their brands and art	Marketing Operations	Art and Collecting	Diverse Range of Cryptocurrencies		Empowered	Transparency
they want to find quick and alternative income sources		they want to collect digital assets	Gaming	Music and Entertainment	Virtual Fashion and Wearables		Smart	Supported
	they want to support artists and creators		Virtual Worlds and Metaverse	Investment Diversification	Social and Community Engagement		Cool	In step with the times

Figure 7.3 MoreNFT meaning before black swan

(EQ1) experience for MoreNFT users. The second aspect of MoreNFT EP concerns the possibility of collecting NFTs (EBB2). MoreNFT offers an exclusive experience (EQ2) compared to both tokenized platforms (e.g., Looksrare) and tokenless NFT platforms (EBK2). Users can access exclusive projects and collections created in collaboration with celebrities or brands.

Additionally, buyers receive certificates and rights to participate in online and offline events without intermediaries. The third aspect concerns the opportunity for creators to craft and release their NFT collections (EBB3). MoreNFT simplifies (EQ3) the NFT creation process directly within their platform. This means that, unlike major NFT marketplaces (EBK3), creators don't need to worry about setting up their own landing page.

Moreover, MoreNFT supports creators in promoting their collections with additional services, including licensed networking, brand ambassador collaborations, web marketing, promotional banners, discord server use, and specialized advertising campaigns. This results in an easier and more convenient (EQ3) process for creators. The final aspect regards the diversification of investment opportunities (EBB3). MoreNFT provides a unique opportunity to diversify investment

EXPERIENTIAL PERFORMANCE		
EXPERIENTIAL BUILDING BLOCKS (EBB)	EXPERIENTIAL QUALITY (EQ)	EXPERIENTIAL BENCHMARK (EBK)
What are the relevant aspects of the customer experience?	In which way do these aspects create more value?	Compared to what substitute/similar experiences?
With **MoreNFT** the user can	How?	Differently from ....
EBB.1 *PERFORM NFT TRANSACTIONS*	In a more REWARDING way In a more EMPOWERING way	TOKENLESS NFT MARKETPLACES TOKENIZED NFT MARKETPLACES
EBB.2 *COLLECT NFTs*	In a more EXCLUSIVE way In a more ENGAGING way	TOKENLESS/TOKENIZED NFT MARKETPLACES
EBB.3 *CRAFT AND RELEASE NFT COLLECTIONS*	In a more CONVENIENT way In an EASIER way	TOKENLESS/TOKENIZED NFT MARKETPLACES
EBB.4 *DIVERSIFY INVESTMENT OPPORTUNITIES*	In a more INDEPENDENT way In more INTERACTIVE way	TRADITIONAL ASSETS

Figure 7.4 MoreNFT experiential performance before black swan

portfolios, distinct from traditional assets (EBK4) such as stocks, bonds, and real estate, more independently and engagingly (EQ4). NFTs can be bought, sold, and traded globally, offering a 24/7 market without intermediaries. Some NFTs also provide interactive and immersive experiences, enhancing the collectors digital interactions (Figure 7.4).

MoreNFT Resources—Before Black Swan

In the MoreNFT business model, the backbone software provides the essential infrastructure for the platform to function. This critical infrastructure enables users to browse, trade, and manage NFTs effortlessly. It ensures secure transactions through smart contracts and seamless blockchain integration while supporting features such as auctions and collections. Additionally, it prioritizes user experience by providing intuitive interfaces and continuous innovation for seamless and captivating platform interaction. Alongside the platform, trading experts are paramount, offering profound insights into NFT market trends, valuation methods, and investment strategies. Another vital resource is the proprietary token—MRN—a digital currency intrinsic to the platform. Tailored to facilitate transactions and incentivize user participation, it may also grant access to exclusive features or benefits

RESOURCES		
PARTNERS	**COMPANY**	**CUSTOMERS**
	Who is in control of these resources?	

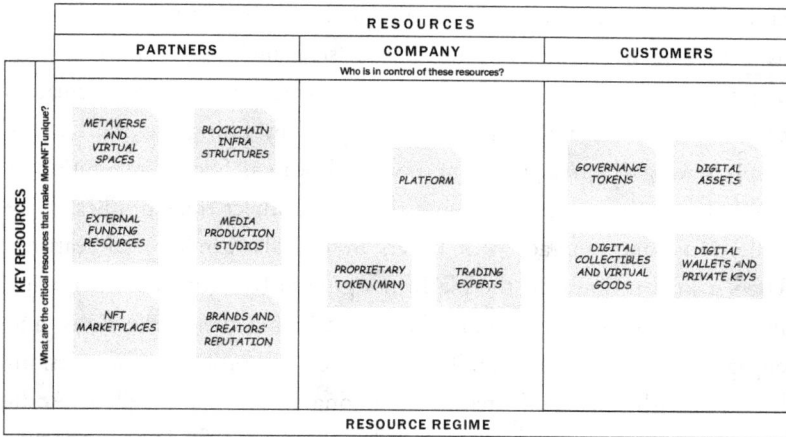

Figure 7.5 MoreNFT resources before black swan

within the ecosystem. Beyond the company's direct control, partnerships with blockchain infrastructures, metaverse, and virtual spaces, and virtual real estate platforms enrich the platform's offerings. Collaborations with established brands, celebrities, and influencers bring unique content, further diversifying the platform's offerings.

Moreover, the support of venture capital firms and investors provides crucial funding, resources, and expertise to propel the growth and development of the NFT platform. Additionally, collaborations with media production studios for NFT-backed media content, such as movies and music, increase the platform's creative potential. Lastly, considering resources controlled by customers themselves, features such as digital wallets and private keys empower users to manage their NFTs and cryptocurrency holdings securely. Users also wield control over their collections, allowing for organization and categorization. Governance tokens allow users to influence decisions through voting mechanisms, ensuring a sense of ownership and community involvement within the MoreNFT ecosystem (Figure 7.5).

MoreNFT Roles—Before Black Swan

In the MoreNFT business model, customers play a central role in key activities on the platform. They're responsible for creating and curating content, whether it be through minting their digital assets as NFTs or building collections. This step includes managing their acquired NFTs and organizing them into portfolios. Moreover, creators can ensure the authenticity of their projects by filling out the Factory form, setting them apart from potential scams. Social integration is another user-driven task, allowing them to connect their profiles, share collections, and interact with others in the platform's social features. Users also contribute to the platform's growth by actively participating in buying, selling, and creating NFTs, enriching their collections, and engaging with the ecosystem. Their feedback and ratings on transactions help establish trust and credibility among creators and sellers. Additionally, users can be advocates for the platform, referring friends and colleagues, further expanding the user base. With governance tokens, users have a say in platform decisions, enabling them to vote on proposals or suggest enhancements to platform rules and features. On the company's side, marketing initiatives are paramount in promoting creators' projects, offering additional services such as licensed networking, brand promotion, and web marketing. Engaging the community through virtual events and exhibitions and partnering with other companies demonstrates a commitment to fostering a vibrant community. Managing the minting process is critical, ensuring an intuitive and user-friendly experience for collectors to tokenize their digital assets. Behind the scenes, the company handles crucial backstage activities such as recruiting creators, celebrities, and brand projects. They also oversee the development of smart contracts, implement secure authentication methods, and monitor the legitimacy of newly minted NFTs. Providing valuable insights and analytics to collectors allows them to make informed decisions about their NFTs' performance. Token burn is a strategic financial activity incentivizing users to hold onto their tokens, potentially leading to price appreciation over time.

Regarding support activities, the company forges partnerships to integrate newly minted NFTs into marketplaces for trading, sale, or auction. They also establish legal frameworks through collaboration with specialized firms, navigating intellectual property issues. Lastly, they define *tokenomics*, which governs the creation, distribution, and

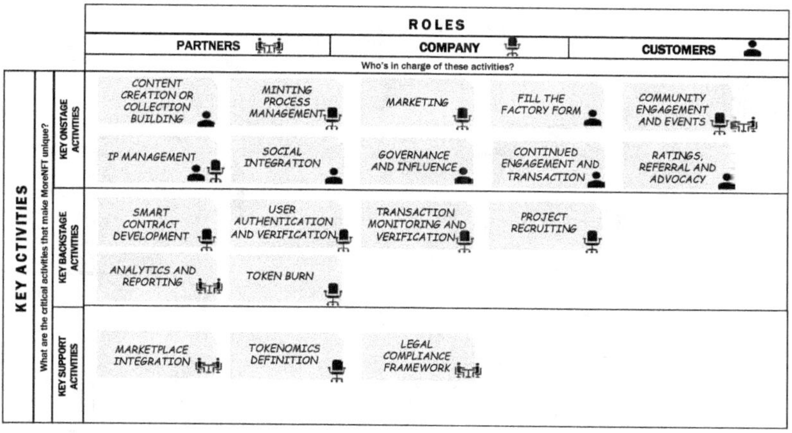
ROLES
PARTNERS
COMPANY
CUSTOMERS
Who's in charge of these activities?
KEY ACTIVITIES
What are the critical activities that make MoreNFT unique?
KEY ONSTAGE ACTIVITIES
CONTENT CREATION OR COLLECTION BUILDING
MINTING PROCESS MANAGEMENT
MARKETING
FILL THE FACTORY FORM
COMMUNITY ENGAGEMENT AND EVENTS
IP MANAGEMENT
SOCIAL INTEGRATION
GOVERNANCE AND INFLUENCE
CONTINUED ENGAGEMENT AND TRANSACTION
RATINGS, REFERRAL AND ADVOCACY
KEY BACKSTAGE ACTIVITIES
SMART CONTRACT DEVELOPMENT
USER AUTHENTICATION AND VERIFICATION
TRANSACTION MONITORING AND VERIFICATION
PROJECT RECRUITING
ANALYTICS AND REPORTING
TOKEN BURN
KEY SUPPORT ACTIVITIES
MARKETPLACE INTEGRATION
TOKENOMICS DEFINITION
LEGAL COMPLIANCE FRAMEWORK

Figure 7.6 MoreNFT roles before black swan

management of tokens within the platform, ensuring a sustainable and rewarding framework for its digital ecosystem (Figure 7.6).

MoreNFT Value Equation—Before Black Swan

The primary customer benefits of the value equation revolve around an exclusive market, granting collectors access to works created by content creators in collaboration with celebrities and brands. Customers also enjoy investment opportunities, rewards for staking and trading, token value appreciation, governance participation, and reduced marketplace fees when using the MRN token. Specifically for creators, the main advantages lie in monetizing digital content, accessing custom marketing services, and gaining exposure to a global audience. This exposure can increase recognition and opportunities in digital art and collectibles. In this way, the platform represents a means to support underrepresented creators and artists from diverse backgrounds, therefore fostering a more inclusive and representative NFT ecosystem. Customers should be aware that efforts are required, including the payment of marketing fees associated with transactions (including minting, buying, and selling NFTs), the need for self-education on NFT operations and crypto jargon, taking precautions to safeguard private keys and wallet information to prevent unauthorized access and potential asset loss,

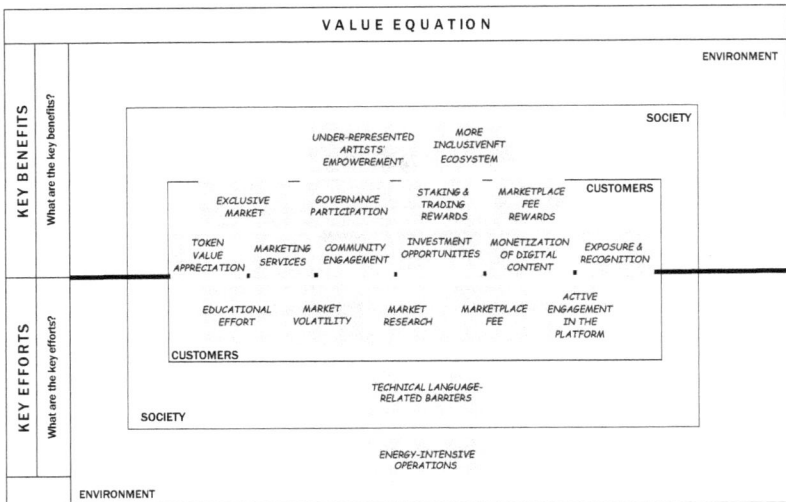

Figure 7.7 MoreNFT value equation before black swan

and understanding the risks tied to possible fluctuations in asset prices. Particularly, overloading users with complex crypto jargon and technical details may create barriers to entry, discouraging potential participants from engaging with the platform. Moreover, the blockchain and NFT space has faced criticism for its energy-intensive processes, which may represent a significant effort, especially for environmentally conscious users (Figure 7.7).

MoreNFT Faces the Black Swan

In November 2022, just as our trio of entrepreneurs was on the verge of launching their platform after more than one year of relentless work, an unforeseen turn of events unfolded. FTX Trading Ltd, one of the largest cryptocurrency exchanges enabling people to trade, buy, and enter into derivative contracts for various coins and tokens, filed for bankruptcy on November 11th. This seismic downfall led to the arrest of FTX's CEO, Sam Bankman-Fried, a 30-year-old MIT graduate heralded as a prodigy of woke capitalism. The CEO faced allegations of imprudent leveraging and mishandling of user funds, compounded by a CoinDesk report raising red flags about FTX's affiliated trading firm, Alameda Research. It was revealed that earlier in 2022, FTX had lent $10 billion from customers' accounts to fund Alameda Research, a move expressly forbidden by FTX's terms of service.

This event was regarded by many as a black swan event due to its unexpected nature, far-reaching consequences, and the appearance of predictability.

First, experts drew parallels between the sudden collapse of FTX and the dynamics underpinning the Lehman Brothers' bankruptcy in 2007, coining it *crypto's Lehman moment*. The CEO of FTX had long been lauded as an example of the positive side of capitalism, and nobody would have anticipated any fraudulent conduct from him. As soon as the report came out, Binance, the largest crypto exchange, swiftly indicated its intentions to divest its holdings of FTX's native crypto, FTT (FTX token), citing transparency concerns. Subsequently, FTX's valuation, which had stood at a substantial $32 billion just a year prior, plummeted, culminating in the filing for bankruptcy protection on November 11th. A staggering $8 billion of FTX customers' funds was estimated to have vanished.

Secondly, the FTX collapse had extreme consequences. The already volatile crypto landscape plummeted below the trillion-dollar mark, shedding billions in value. In less than 24 hours, between November 7th and 8th, cryptocurrencies experienced a sharp 22 percent decline. Tether, a stablecoin, slipped below its established peg price of $1.00, settling at $0.97, while Bitcoin plummeted to its lowest valuation in two years. Reverberations of this crash were severe, with many funds and investors grappling with their own crises as they incurred losses, wrote off investments, and witnessed users exiting the market. Bloomberg reported that the collapse of FTX amplified institutional skepticism regarding cryptocurrencies as a viable asset class, casting a shadow on the credibility of an entire industry. Besides the financial repercussions, the fallout also bore political implications. FTX CEO Sam Bankman-Fried had been the poster child of *effective altruism* (EA), a global movement focused on maximizing positive impact and helping others that attracted numerous billionaires and politicians who justified their affluence to serve others better and exert positive change. Despite leaders of the EA movement condemning FTX's actions, the loss of trust (and funding) in the movement's philanthropic entities linked to the exchange was undeniable.

Finally, in hindsight, the predictability of FTX's collapse became apparent. In the aftermath, it became clear that crypto assets could have suddenly imploded, and unregulated exchanges like FTX were ill-suited for safeguarding funds. The investigations brought to light a disturbing level of mismanagement within the organization. This was marked by a leadership team lacking experience and a pervasive breakdown in corporate controls across all levels. One striking issue was the absence of essential financial statements, indicative of a broader failure in internal management practices.

Now, let's turn our attention back to our trio of entrepreneurs. In the wake of the FTX collapse and the ensuing market turmoil, the future of MoreNFT hung in the balance. It became evident to them that the crisis had a natural ripple effect on the value of NFTs. Even though lower crypto prices made NFTs cheaper, buyers were hesitant, and holders were reluctant to sell at a loss. Investors decided to keep their NFTs safe by moving them off exchanges and centralized platforms, allowing the storm to pass. Given these circumstances, our entrepreneurs recognized that the present moment wasn't optimal for launching a new NFT marketplace, let alone introducing a proprietary token, the MRN. They knew a pivot was inevitable, so they took a moment to regroup and plan their next steps. Here's a hint: what came next was a bold repurposing plan, one that would completely transform their business model and redefine their path forward.

MoreNFT After the Black Swan

Following the FTX black swan event, trust in the cryptocurrency industry plummeted, casting a dark cloud over MoreNFT's once-promising business model. The impact was severe, and it became evident that introducing the MRN token, a cornerstone of their strategy, was no longer feasible. As the reality sunk in, the trio behind MoreNFT found themselves at a crossroads. The unexpected setback dampened their initial excitement, and the temptation to abandon the project was strong. However, they couldn't overlook the countless hours of hard work—the sleepless nights and weekends spent with their developers perfecting the platform. Walking away wasn't an option. With renewed determination, they assessed their remaining assets. If the token was no longer viable, what did they still have? The answer was clear: the platform itself. Over the past year, they had poured their hearts into its development, and it had become their most valuable asset.

This realization marked a turning point for MoreNFT. Faced with adversity, they set out to rethink their key resources. While the Black Swan event had taken one crucial element off the table—the token, their well-built platform was still intact and ready to be used in new, creative ways.

In Chapter 3, as we discuss into how to initiate a BML logic transformation by *sharing resources* (the third element of the BML), you may recall that sharing resources implies not only reclaiming some key resources controlled by external partners or customers (referred to as "*Insharing*") but also in externalizing them to partners or users (referred to as "*Outsharing*"). The key resource to initiate a sharing practice was evidently the platform. Since it was initially under the company's control, the challenge was deciding who it should be shared with. Initially designed to empower creators, the original MoreNFT platform provided the tools to create NFTs and utilize them as a key for accessing exclusive experiences reserved for the owners. By crafting and selling branded NFTs, they could engage with their audience in innovative ways. For instance, they could release limited edition NFTs linked to their products, events, or campaigns. In a moment when NFT trading volumes have decreased following the implosion of FTX, they can still be an excellent marketing vehicle. This idea was corroborated by the observation that, despite the crypto downturn, consumer brands—a significant portion of their original MoreNFT market—continued to venture into the NFT space, viewing it as an alternative and innovative marketing approach to reach younger generations. Companies such as Nike, Reddit, Sony, and others announced new products utilizing NFTs for digital collectibles.

This led MoreNFT founders to transform their BML by sharing their platform with brands. As a result, they decided to transition

MoreNFT into a white-label business model by licensing their platform to companies. The licensees can then customize the platform with their own branding and offer it to their customers, allowing them to engage, reward, and monetize in unprecedented ways. This shift to a white-label model can be seen as a way of externalizing a key resource to customers. In this arrangement, MoreNFT furnishes a platform that can be rebranded and presented by another company as if it were its own. This enables the purchasing company to access and employ the service without in-house development. Essentially, MoreNFT is externalizing its technology to be utilized by another entity under its own brand. But let's proceed in order.

By employing the TST tool to analyze this case study, we can observe that MoreNFT initiates its BML transformation through a *sharing* practice. The MoreNFT team strategically transferred the control of one of the key resources—the platform—which was previously conceived to be managed exclusively by their company in the old business model, directly to the brands (Figure 7.8.)

Starting from this simple *sharing* maneuver, a whole redefinition of the *resource regime* unfolds in the MoreNFT BML. This encompasses eliminating and introducing new key resources and redistributing their control among the company, customers, and partners.

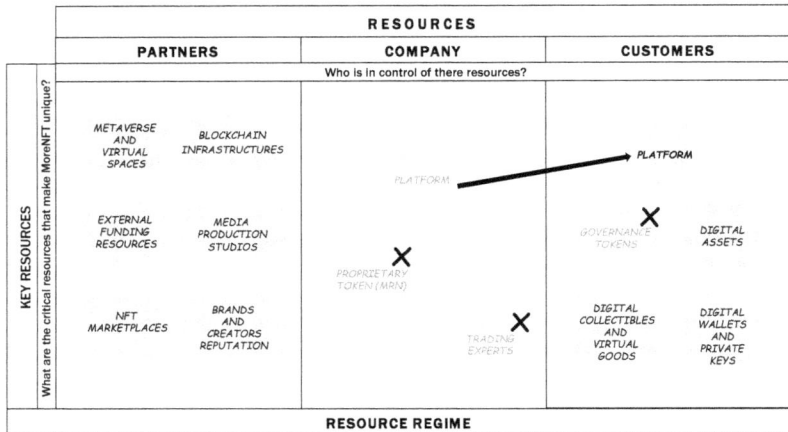

Figure 7.8 MoreNFT—BML transformation by sharing the resources

MoreNFT Resources After the Black Swan

In the new business model, specific resources traditionally associated with NFT trading, such as traders and proprietary tokens, are no longer essential. Additionally, collaborations with established brands will shift from being partnerships to becoming customer relationships.

Meanwhile, the backbone software of the platform will take center stage in the realm of the company's resources, ensuring a scalable infrastructure and compliance with crucial legal and regulatory requirements for NFTs. Customization and branding tools will empower clients to personalize and rebrand the platform to their specifications. The platform will continue to offer essential features such as minting and marketplace functionality, providing the necessary tools and infrastructure. Moreover, it will furnish standardized legal documentation, including contracts and terms of service, which can be tailored to meet individual client needs. Salespeople will be pivotal in client acquisition, solution presentation, and product knowledge transfer. They will be instrumental in guiding clients through the process. In this white-label NFT platform model, partners may also control key resources, such as blockchain infrastructure, legal and compliance expertise, and advanced security solutions (Figure 7.9).

MoreNFT Roles After the Black Swan

Roles have undergone a transformation in the new white-label NFT platform model. Onstage activities now include crucial sales efforts and practical product demonstrations necessitated by the product's complexity. Client onboarding and training have become vital for educating clients and their teams on effectively utilizing and managing the platform. The client assumes responsibility for customizing, rebranding, promoting, and managing content, collections, and metadata associated with their specific NFTs. This includes defining minting parameters royalties and customizing marketplace features tailored to their particular use case. At the backstage level, core activities revolve around continuous refinement and enhancement of the NFT platform.

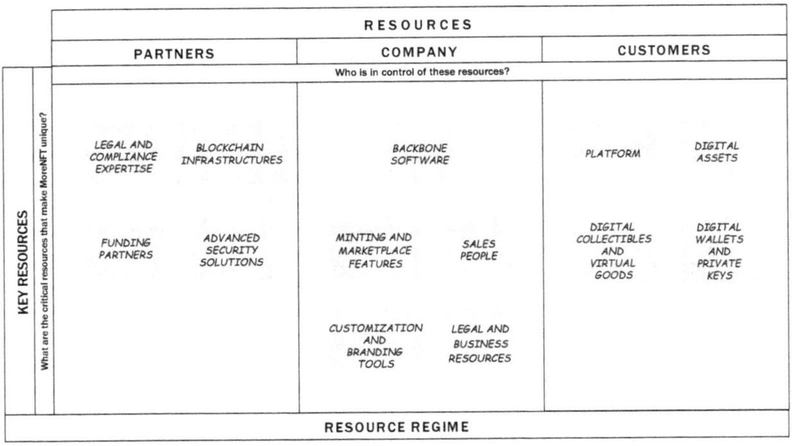
RESOURCES
PARTNERS
COMPANY
CUSTOMERS
Who is in control of these resources?
KEY RESOURCES
What are the critical resources that make MoreNFT unique?
LEGAL AND COMPLIANCE EXPERTISE
BLOCKCHAIN INFRASTRUCTURES
FUNDING PARTNERS
ADVANCED SECURITY SOLUTIONS
BACKBONE SOFTWARE
MINTING AND MARKETPLACE FEATURES
SALES PEOPLE
CUSTOMIZATION AND BRANDING TOOLS
LEGAL AND BUSINESS RESOURCES
PLATFORM
DIGITAL ASSETS
DIGITAL COLLECTIBLES AND VIRTUAL GOODS
DIGITAL WALLETS AND PRIVATE KEYS
RESOURCE REGIME

Figure 7.9 MoreNFT resources after black swan

This encompasses tasks such as smart contract development, seamless blockchain integration, and user interface design.

Additionally, providing tools and guidance for clients to customize the platform with their brand identity and preferences has gained significance. Designing tools and dashboards to monitor user engagement, transaction volume, and other pertinent metrics has become a pivotal backstage activity. Moreover, managing the metadata storage system's initial setup and ongoing maintenance is essential. Support activities include the creation of guides and tutorials to facilitate effective navigation of the platform. Continuous innovation and research have emerged as critical activities, ensuring alignment with industry trends, emerging technologies, and user feedback for sustained product improvement. Partnerships with specialist consultants have also gained prominence, particularly in implementing security measures and tailoring legal documentation to meet specific local or industry regulations (Figure 7.10).

MoreNFT Experiential Performance After Black Swan

The new EP is founded on new EBBs. It offers a novel approach, allowing for custom, swift, user-friendly, and independent NFT creation compared to existing NFT publishers and marketplaces. Thanks to

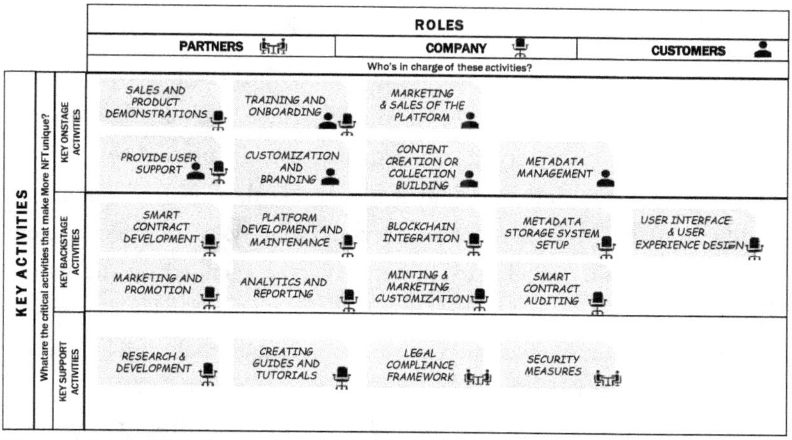

ROLES		
PARTNERS	**COMPANY**	**CUSTOMERS**
	Who's in charge of these activities?	

KEY ACTIVITIES — What are the critical activities that make More NFT unique?

KEY ONSTAGE ACTIVITIES

PARTNERS		COMPANY		CUSTOMERS
SALES AND PRODUCT DEMONSTRATIONS	TRAINING AND ONBOARDING	MARKETING & SALES OF THE PLATFORM		
PROVIDE USER SUPPORT	CUSTOMIZATION AND BRANDING	CONTENT CREATION OR COLLECTION BUILDING	METADATA MANAGEMENT	

KEY BACKSTAGE ACTIVITIES

SMART CONTRACT DEVELOPMENT	PLATFORM DEVELOPMENT AND MAINTENANCE	BLOCKCHAIN INTEGRATION	METADATA STORAGE SYSTEM SETUP	USER INTERFACE & USER EXPERIENCE DESIGN
MARKETING AND PROMOTION	ANALYTICS AND REPORTING	MINTING & MARKETING CUSTOMIZATION	SMART CONTRACT AUDITING	

KEY SUPPORT ACTIVITIES

RESEARCH & DEVELOPMENT	CREATING GUIDES AND TUTORIALS	LEGAL COMPLIANCE FRAMEWORK	SECURITY MEASURES

Figure 7.10 MoreNFT roles after black swan

the white-label business model and an intuitive interface, customers can effortlessly design and personalize one or more NFT collections within minutes, even without specific tech skills such as coding or blockchain expertise. One remarkable feature is the seamless integration of specific use cases into NFTs. These can encompass a range of utilities that a brand's customers can access after acquiring an NFT, including entry to offline and online events, participation in surveys, giveaways, redeemable physical products, exclusive content downloads, and discounts/promotional codes—all directly from the platform. This capability fosters deeper community engagement, surpassing traditional Web 2.0 marketing by establishing more profound customer relationships.

Furthermore, the platform grants brands ownership, access, and customer data management reducing reliance on external channels. Lastly, MoreNFT enables brands to connect with younger audiences like Gen Z, often considered challenging to reach. They allocate less time to social media and more to ad-free gaming and streaming platforms, valuing community-centered relationships over traditional company–client interactions (Figure 7.11).

MoreNFT Value Equation After the Black Swan

With the reconfigured BML, the value proposition transforms, unlocking new advantages for customers. These include the capacity to tailor and brand the NFT marketplace to align precisely with their unique preferences and brand identity. Access to advanced features is readily available, offering enhanced functionality. Customers benefit from a significantly accelerated time-to-market, enabled by the white-label solution's prebuilt framework, eliminating the need for extensive technical skills or blockchain expertise to launch their NFT marketplace. This newfound efficiency brings about greater cost-effectiveness, sparing them the arduous task of building a platform from the ground up.

Moreover, customers retain complete ownership and control over the data generated within their NFT marketplace, ensuring data autonomy. This, in turn, promotes fair compensation practices by ensuring that creators receive a reasonable share of the proceeds from their work. This can help address concerns related to exploitation and inequality within the creative industry. Conversely, the revised value equation

EXPERIENTIAL PERFORMANCE		
EXPERIENTIAL BUILDING BLOCKS (EBB)	EXPERIENTIAL QUALITY (EQ)	EXPERIENTIAL BENCHMARK (EBK)
What are the relevant aspects of the customer experience?	In which way do these aspects create more value?	Compared to what substitute/similar experiences?
With **MoreNFT** the user can	How?	Differently from ....
EBB.1 *CRAFT AND RELEASE NFT COLLECTIONS*	In an EASIER way In a FASTER way In a more CUSTOM way In a more INDEPENDENT way	NFT PUBLISHERS / NFT MARKETPLACES
EBB.2 *INCORPORATE SPECIFIC USE CASES INTO NFTS*	In a more INTEGRATED way	NFT PUBLISHERS / NFT MARKETPLACES
EBB.3 *ENGAGE THE COMMUNITY*	In a more EFFECTIVE way In a more REWARDING way In a more EMPOWERING way	NFT PUBLISHERS / NFT MARKETPLACES WEB 2.0 MARKETING
EBB.4 *REACH A YOUNGER AUDIENCE*	In a more EFFECTIVE way In more INNOVATIVE way	WEB 2.0 MARKETING

Figure 7.11 MoreNFT experiential performance after black swan

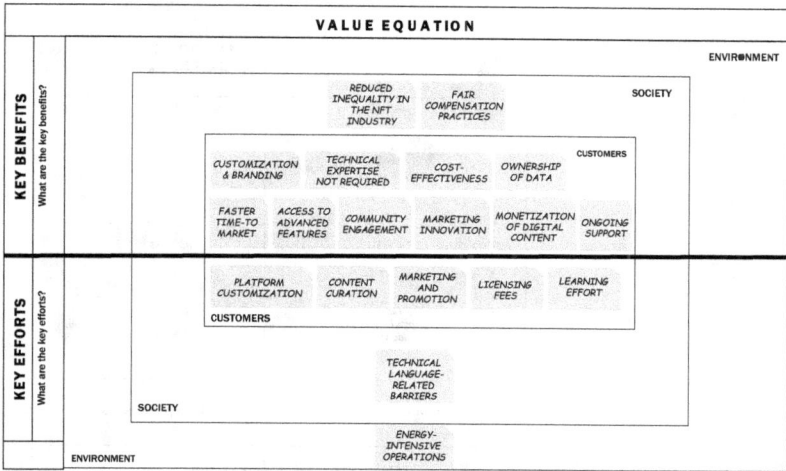

Figure 7.12 MoreNFT value equation after the black swan

introduces additional efforts, including the time invested in customizing the platform to harmonize with their brand—a process encompassing design adjustments and feature configurations. Content curation, licensing fee management, marketing and promotional endeavors, and the need to familiarize themselves with the platform's array of features and tools all contribute to the effort required for a successful venture (Figure 7.12).

MoreNFT Meaning After the Black Swan

Presented as a solution for brands seeking to revolutionize their marketing through web3 and digital assets, the new meaning of MoreNFT's white label is rooted in innovative end-uses. These include expediting entry into the NFT market, diversifying revenue streams through digital asset monetization, gaining greater control over customer data, and accessing new markets—most notably, Gen Z. Additionally, it leads to heightened customer engagement. The usage context of this new meaning extends to strategic repositioning, rebranding maneuvers, and community engagement initiatives. The symbolic significance of this transformation is amplified by the

MEANING						
END-USE		USAGE CONTEXT			SYMBOLIC SIGNIFICANCE	
For which purposes did people use MoreNFT?		In association with which other experiences MoreNFT was seen as relevant?			What feelings and emotions did MoreNFT evoke?	
Clients use MoreNFT when ...		Clients use MoreNFT with ...			Clients use MoreNFT to feel ...	
they want to enter the NFT market quickly	they want their marketing through web3		Strategic repositioning	Rebranding	empowered	transparency
they want to find alternative revenue streams	they want to exploit customer data	Offline marketing	Product diversification	Community engagement initiatives	smart	assisted
they want to reach new markets	they want to increase customer engagement	Virtual worlds and metaverse	New products' launch		efficient	in step with the times

People love MoreNFT because *they not only let you in the NFT world but also let you keep the keys!*

Figure 7.13 MoreNFT meaning after the black swan

efficiency and empowerment that MoreNFT provides. Its tools enable the seamless design and personalization of one or more NFT collections within minutes, allowing for autonomous management in the web3 landscape—a realm once reserved for highly specialized tech companies. As a result, the newfound reason why people love MoreNFT crystallizes into this: *they not only let you in the NFT world but also let you keep the keys!* (Figure 7.13).

So What?

The MoreNFT story exemplifies the potential of adopting a resilient mindset in the face of adversity, emerging even stronger. The journey of our entrepreneurial trio showcases the transformative power of embracing change, even when it necessitates letting go of something deeply cherished and taking a step back. When the unexpected black swan event threatened to disrupt their project, they didn't simply accept the setback. Instead, they thoroughly evaluated their existing BML. They took proactive steps to recognize that key resources, particularly the token, were no longer viable in light of the black swan's impact. They embarked on a brainstorming process, leveraging the resources at their disposal to initiate a transformative shift in their resource strategy (BML transformation through sharing the resources). This exemplifies what we refer to as TST—a willingness to experiment and innovate fearlessly.

Chapter Overview

In this chapter, we illustrate the second of the three managerial challenges likely to affect companies' current logic of value creation: black swan events. These events possess three defining characteristics: unpredictability, as they are unforeseeable outliers with no precedent; extreme impact, causing widespread and severe consequences; and hindsight illumination, leading us to believe we should have foreseen them only after they occur. Black swan events can bring both challenges and opportunities. The TST tool can be used as a training method to deal with unforeseen events and turn them into opportunities. It provides a practical three-step process: understanding the black swan event's impact on the industry, analyzing current BML vulnerabilities, and experimenting with new iterations based on identified vulnerabilities. This mindset empowers businesses to turn potential threats into avenues for growth and innovation. The chapter culminates in an analysis of MoreNFT, showcasing the power of embracing change, even when it means letting go of something cherished and taking a step back.

CHAPTER 8

Paradox Management

What Will You Learn in This Chapter?

You will:

- Understand what are the implications of pursuing a paradox management strategy.
- Learn how paradox management affects a Business Model Logic (BML).
- Understand how to pursue a paradox management strategy by using the Transformative Strategic Thinking (TST) tool.
- Understand the implications of adopting a TST approach to pursue a paradox management strategy from a real-world business case.

Challenge #3 Paradox Management: Bridging Contradictions for Business Success

In the ever-changing business world, managers often find themselves caught in a web of complex decisions. They grapple with questions that tug them in different directions. Should they steer toward change, pushing boundaries and embracing new frontiers? Or should they anchor in stability, preserving what's tried and true? Is it better to cater to local markets, tailoring offerings to specific tastes, or opt for a standardized global approach?

These dilemmas paint a picture of a manager's role today—no longer just problem-solvers but navigators of paradoxes. Unlike straightforward issues, these paradoxes don't have easy answers. They present seemingly opposing choices, yet are both crucial and often interdependent. Take, for instance, the apparent conflict between cost reduction and quality improvement. While on the surface, they may seem incompatible, in reality, cost-reduction efforts frequently entail enhancements in operational efficiency and processes, which can yield higher quality outputs. Relying solely on traditional *either/or* thinking falls short in navigating this intricate landscape.

In response to the escalating complexity and interdependence of strategic challenges, scholars from diverse disciplines such as organizational psychology, management studies, and leadership theory have rallied to shape the theory of paradox management.

The theory of paradox management recognizes that, in today's intricate organizational environments, embracing and leveraging the strengths of both ends of each paradox is critical to effective leadership and decision making, as these opposing goals can often reinforce each other, ultimately driving a more robust and competitive business strategy.

This approach calls for a shift from *either/or* to *both/and* thinking. It means finding ways to harmonize seemingly conflicting strategic goals. Whether it's the delicate dance between change and stability, the tightrope walk of innovation and efficiency, or the balance of profit and social responsibility, embracing paradoxes fosters adaptability and resilience in today's fast-paced business landscape.

Take a look at Toyota's incredible journey, an excellent example of handling conflicting challenges. Through their renowned Toyota Production System (TPS), they deftly balance innovation and operational efficiency. This system, rooted in lean manufacturing, waste reduction, and a culture of constant improvement, has allowed them to achieve outstanding operational efficiency while still fostering an environment of innovation.

Moreover, Toyota's global success is rooted in its ability to customize products to local markets. They understand that consumer preferences and needs vary from region to region. By tailoring their offerings, they have maintained a strong presence in diverse markets worldwide. Toyota's strategic approach highlights that it's possible for companies, even in a complex and competitive industry like automotive, to manage paradoxes effectively. Toyota has sustained long-term success and a solid reputation by striking a balance between innovation and efficiency and by customizing offerings for different markets while competing globally.

On the flip side, consider the case of Volkswagen, a company that struggled with effectively handling paradoxes. One of their major stumbling blocks was finding the right balance between short-term financial gains and the long-term management of their brand reputation. Probably, some of you will remember the *Dieselgate* scandal that involved the German car manufacturer in 2015. Under pressure to meet immediate financial targets and regulatory standards, Volkswagen installed software in their diesel vehicles to mislead emissions tests. These devices were designed to detect when the car was undergoing emissions testing in a lab environment and, during those times, activate emissions control systems to reduce pollutants. In real-world driving conditions, however, the vehicles emitted significantly higher levels of nitrogen oxides (NOx), a group of pollutants that contribute to smog and respiratory problems. The cars were emitting up to 40 times the allowable limit of NOx. The deception was uncovered by researchers at the International Council on Clean Transportation (ICCT) and West Virginia University. They conducted independent emissions tests on Volkswagen diesel vehicles and found discrepancies between lab results and on-road emissions. While yielding short-term benefits, this decision severely damaged Volkswagen's long-term brand integrity and customer trust. The scandal had far-reaching consequences, affecting approximately 11 million vehicles across various Volkswagen brands worldwide. It led to widespread public outrage, legal actions, and a sharp drop in Volkswagen's stock value. The case underscores the critical importance of effectively managing the paradox between short-term financial gains and the preservation of long-term brand equity. It's a sobering lesson on the dangers of compromising a long-term reputation for quick wins.

Key Takeaways

- In today's fast-paced business environment, managers regularly confront complex decisions entailing conflicting priorities.
- In business leadership, a paradox refers to a set of objectives or challenges that initially seem incompatible, presenting a seemingly binary either/or choice.
- These paradoxes present options that are not only contradictory but also intricately interconnected.
- Effectively navigating these paradoxes demands the ability to embrace and capitalize on the strengths inherent in both sides, shifting from a restrictive either/or mindset to a more expansive both/and approach.
- Failing to navigate these paradoxes adeptly can result in a loss of competitiveness and, in extreme cases, even lead to business failure.

Understanding How Paradox Management Affects Business Model Logics

In this chapter, we discuss paradox management—the ability of navigating conflicting objectives through a both/and leadership approach.

Common management paradoxes encompass areas such as innovation (balancing the present with the future, existing offerings with new ventures, and stability with change), globalization (balancing global interconnectivity with local needs, breadth with depth, and collaboration with competition), and obligation (balancing social impact with profitability).

For instance, consider the innovation paradox faced by IBM in the late 1990s. Senior managers recognized the imperative of leveraging Internet technology for the company's future while preserving its traditional strength in client-server markets. Executing both strategies called for distinct structures, cultures, rewards, and metrics, presenting a challenge in simultaneous implementation. This endeavor involved reconciling conflicts among executives, as proponents of the old and advocates of the new, each grappled with a perceived threat to their professional identity.

Another intriguing example lies in the globalization paradox experienced by NASA in 2009. The human health and performance director sought to drive collaborative, cross-disciplinary research to generate new knowledge. However, he encountered resistance from scientists who were protective of their domains and attached to their roles as independent researchers. As technology enabled more open, collaborative research, NASA's scientists paradoxically grew more apprehensive about the recognition of their individual contributions. The creation of novel ideas demanded both collaboration and independent work, yet these approaches were organizationally and culturally at odds.

Furthermore, the obligation paradox was exemplified by Unilever's CEO in 2010. He launched the Unilever Sustainable Living Plan, aiming to double the company's size by 2020, all while enhancing the well-being of over a billion individuals and decreasing the company's environmental footprint. The underlying assumption was that long-term investments in social and environmental initiatives would ultimately lead to greater profits. However, the CEO encountered resistance from senior team leaders who experienced heightened anxiety and contention over resource allocation, highlighting the tension between short-term profits and broader societal and environmental goals. A pivotal aspect of effective paradox management lies in its departure from the pursuit of stability and predictability. Instead, paradoxical leadership thrives on dynamism and welcomes change. This approach places a premium on experimentation and acknowledges the invaluable lessons that stem from failures. These experiences generate vital feedback loops, fostering continuous learning and adaptations.

As a result, managing paradoxes and balancing conflicting goals often requires creative thinking and questioning established assumptions. This can lead to significant changes or even a complete transformation of the existing business model. Take McDonald's, often seen as a symbol of globalization. The U.S. fast-food giant has grappled with the challenge of maintaining a globally recognizable brand while also catering to local tastes, preferences, and cultural nuances across its worldwide presence. In 1993, McDonald's took a significant step by opening the first McCafé in Melbourne. This marked a departure from the traditional McDonald's concept, as it was designed to align with Australian consumers' unique tastes and preferences. Australia is one of the world's leading consumers of coffee per capita. The McCafé retained the fast-food ethos while introducing a fresh range of food and beverages and a more inviting interior design. This innovative move is still considered one of the company's most successful business model adaptations. From its inaugural location on Swanson Street in Melbourne, the McCafé concept quickly gained traction and became a global phenomenon. Today, it operates over 4,000 stores across 60 countries. In 2021, McDonald's took another step by launching a McCafé blend, roasted in Melbourne and sourced from farms certified by the Rainforest Alliance in Brazil, Honduras, Kenya, and Ethiopia.

The McCafé business model innovation exemplifies the effectiveness of adopting a TST approach when implementing a paradox management strategy. By balancing conflicting goals with a creative and experimental mindset, businesses can catalyze transformative shifts in their business models, creating a self-reinforcing innovation cycle.

In the context of paradoxical management, using the TST tool involves a simple three-step process.

Step 1. Analyze the Current Business Model Logic

Leverage the TST framework to dissect and deconstruct your BML. This analytical step is crucial for obtaining a comprehensive grasp of the underlying assumptions driving your business model. Scrutinize each element of your BML—encompassing *meaning, EP, resources, roles*, and *value equation*.

Step 2. Pinpoint the Polarized Elements

Explicitly define the two conflicting goals representing the poles of your paradox (e.g., profit and social impact). Evaluate each element of your BML and, by paying particular attention to their subdimensions, assess which ones exhibit a stronger inclination toward one goal over the other.

Step 3. Experiment With a New Business Model Logic

Identify and prioritize elements with the most pronounced polarity. Use them as a starting point for transforming your BML. The opposing goal should guide each refinement. For instance, in the pursuit of balancing profit and social objectives, if the key activities in your BML's roles predominantly align with profit goals, initiate a switching practice aimed at reorienting those activities toward social impact. Conversely, if you discover that your key resources prioritize social sustainability but are cost-intensive (not profit-driven), kickstart a sharing practice focused on rendering those key resources more cost-effective. After adjusting other elements, compare alternative BMLs to evaluate their potential in balancing the paradox. Iterate the process until a consistent and balanced BML is achieved (Figure 8.1).

Applying TST to Managing Paradoxes: The Case of Congo Clothing Company (CCC)

CCC Before Managing the Paradoxes

To understand the impact of embracing TST to navigate management paradoxes, let's follow the journey of a passionate young entrepreneur named Milain, whose mission was to leverage entrepreneurship to drive meaningful change. Born in Congo, Milain crisscrossed Africa in his youth before finding himself in Paris for high school. His first steps into entrepreneurship took place at the University of Miami when he launched an online skincare brand for dark skin and ventured into property tech. Having grown up relocating across various African nations and receiving an education abroad, Milain's allegiance has always remained closely tied to Congo. In 2018, he learned that Congolese

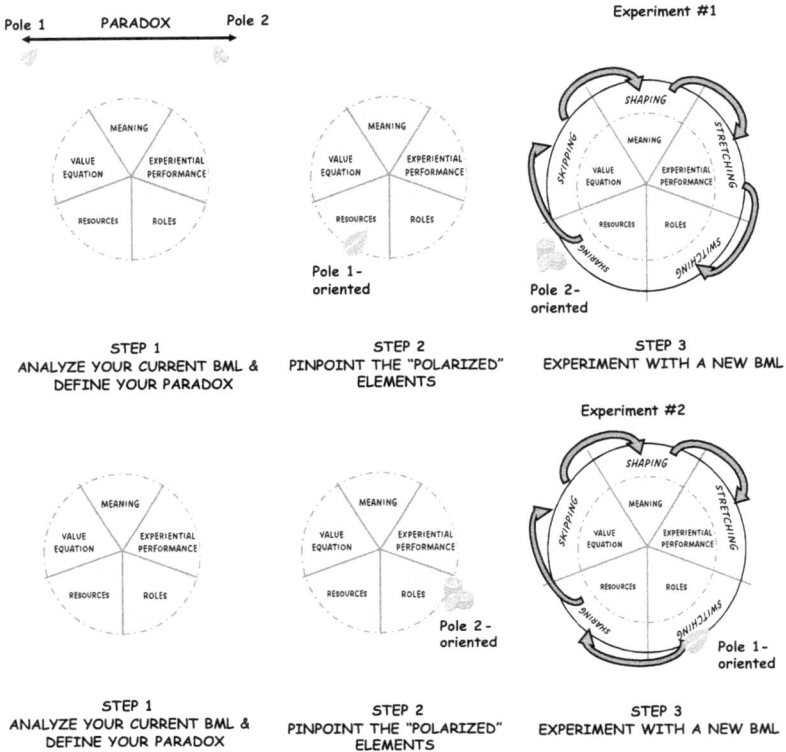

Figure 8.1 *Using the TST tool to managing paradoxes*

doctor Denis Mukwege won a share of the Nobel Peace Prize. Milain, waking up early in Miami to watch Mukwege's speech in Norway, felt an overwhelming pride for his homeland. In his speech, Mukwege shares his experience as a founder of the Panzi Foundation, which helps women who survived sexual violence, painting a poignant picture of the plight of countless women who endured unspeakable suffering during Congo's civil wars, fueled by corruption and conflict for critical minerals. This speech had a profound impact on Milain, shaping his entrepreneurial journey. It strengthened his conviction that this issue requires more focus, and he believes that entrepreneurship can be a powerful force for change, especially as younger generations become more conscious of their consumption habits. However, something about that speech surprised him: "It only had a handful of views on YouTube," making him feel like it hadn't reached the broader audience it deserved.

Milain spent a year trying to meet Mukwege, eventually tracking him down in Los Angeles in 2019. Here, he shared his vision of leveraging conscious consumerism in Western markets to amplify Mukwege's message.

Meanwhile, he moved to Boston to study Political Sciences at MIT, where he found the support he needed to launch his new venture, Congo Clothing Company (CCC), with the dual scope of raising awareness about the story of women in Congo but also selling its value offering. CCC is a fashion brand with a denim clothing line that seamlessly blends Congo-inspired designs with a universal, cross-border appeal. Its social purpose is twofold: to provide survivors with a source of income while sharing their powerful stories. CCC donates 10 percent of its profits to the Panzi Foundation to train and upskill survivors of sexual violence in the Democratic Republic of Congo (DRC), helping them embark on a recovery journey. CCC converts each purchase into the equivalent number of days of training provided. A complete training program is 180 days and costs $100 to operate. By purchasing this brand, consumers not only support DRC survivors but also become part of a narrative that educates and empowers them. The CCC platform is indeed conceived as a platform to raise awareness about the violence in DRC.

The choice of fashion as the medium is deliberate, as it allows the message to be absorbed, embraced, and shared. However, Milain understands that having a noble mission and a powerful message isn't enough. Consumers need something they genuinely like and find cool. Therefore, he decided to harness creativity to reconcile the divide between style and social impact. That's why CCC places special emphasis on design, incorporating Congo-style colors and decorations with a Western flair. The company's logo, a zigzag between two straight lines, symbolizes the fusion of an ancient Congolese Kingdom (the zigzag) with a Western aesthetic (the straight lines).

Additionally, CCC provides a platform for women in Congo to shape clothing design actively. Through CCC's proprietary app, they can submit their creative work, which CCC compensates through licensing fees. Besides allocating a portion of the profits to the training programs,

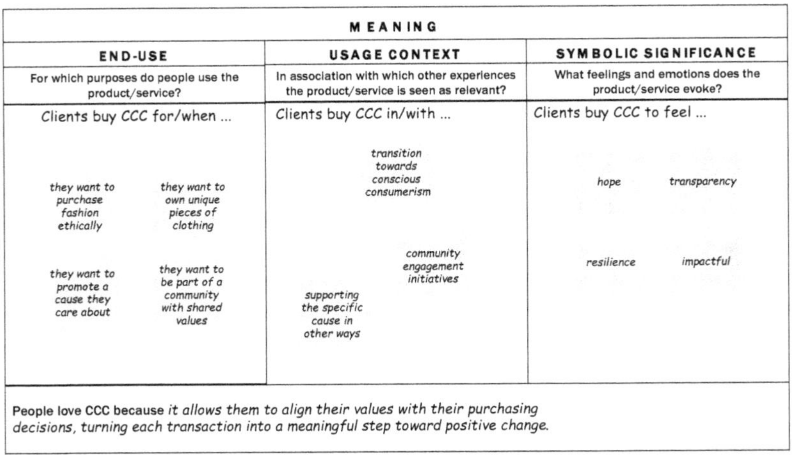

MEANING		
END-USE	**USAGE CONTEXT**	**SYMBOLIC SIGNIFICANCE**
For which purposes do people use the product/service?	In association with which other experiences the product/service is seen as relevant?	What feelings and emotions does the product/service evoke?
Clients buy CCC for/when ...	Clients buy CCC in/with ...	Clients buy CCC to feel ...
they want to purchase fashion ethically	they want to own unique pieces of clothing	transition towards conscious consumerism	hope transparency
they want to promote a cause they care about	they want to be part of a community with shared values	supporting the specific cause in other ways community engagement initiatives	resilience impactful
People love CCC because *it allows them to align their values with their purchasing decisions, turning each transaction into a meaningful step toward positive change.*		

Figure 8.2 Meaning before managing the paradoxes

CCC supports the purchase of individual sewing machines for the survivors to grant them a degree of autonomy and self-sufficiency. The following sections provide a more detailed illustration of the CCC BML.

CCC Meaning Before Managing the Paradoxes

CCC stands as a beacon of conscious fashion, offering a diverse range of clothing items, from denims and jackets to t-shirts and accessories, each meticulously designed to seamlessly blend Western aesthetics with the vibrant culture and hues of Congo. Every piece carries nuanced style details that echo a powerful message. It's this fusion that entices people to choose CCC, seeking unique, style-defining additions that celebrate both individuality and cultural appreciation. Beyond being a fashion destination, CCC's platform serves as an informational hub, educating customers about the cause and illustrating the tangible impact of their purchases. This dual purpose compels individuals to choose CCC not just for style but as a conscious act of support for a vital social cause. Moreover, CCC fosters a sense of community through engaging events, from vibrant parties to enlightening talks. These gatherings serve as a gateway for individuals to deepen their understanding of the cause, offering yet another compelling reason to stand behind the CCC brand (meaning end-use).

CCC products find their place not only in the transition toward conscious consumerism but also in the broader spectrum of supporting the cause in other ways (meaning usage context). At its core, CCC's mission is to transform consumerism into a force for good. By using fashion as a medium to shed light on the plight of sexual violence in the DRC and providing a robust reporting system to track the impact of purchases, CCC embodies hope, resilience, and impactful change (meaning symbolic significance). Ultimately, people love CCC because *it allows them to align their values with purchasing decisions, turning each transaction into a meaningful step toward positive change (Figure 8.2).*

CCC Experiential Performance Before Managing the Paradoxes

CCC EP is built upon three fundamental EBBs (Figure 8.3). The first gives the possibility of buying fashion items by directing a portion of each purchase toward fighting violence against women in Congo (EBB1). This not only imbues the act with greater significance and reward but also sets CCC apart from other fashion brands (EBK1) through its unique collections inspired by Congo culture (EQ1).

EXPERIENTIAL PERFORMANCE		
EXPERIENTIAL BUILDING BLOCKS (EBB)	**EXPERIENTIAL QUALITY (EQ)**	**EXPERIENTIAL BENCHMARK (EBK)**
What are the relevant aspects of the customer experience?	In which way do these aspects create more value?	Compared to what substitute, "similar experiences?
With *CCC* the user can	How?	Differently from ....
EBB.1 PURCHASE FASHION ITEMS	In a more IMPACTFUL way / In a more DIFFERENTIATED way / In a more REWARDING way	REGULAR FASHION BRANDS
EBB.2 TRACK THE IMPACT OF THEIR PURCHASES	In an EASIER way / In a more TRANSPARENT way / In a more ENTERTAINING way	CONSCIOUS FASHION BRANDS
EBB.3 SUPPORT A CAUSE THEY CARE ABOUT	In a more ENGAGED way / In a more INFORMED way / In a more REWARDING way	DONATIONS

Figure 8.3 CCC Experiential performance before managing the paradoxes

The second aspect of EP empowers consumers to track the tangible impact of their purchases (EBB2). Through a tracking system, buyers gain insight into how their contributions translate into training days. This experience is enhanced by a gamification element that ranks and rewards customers based on their collective impact, providing a more transparent and enjoyable engagement (EQ2) than other conscious brands (EBK2).

Finally, customers not only acquire a stylish fashion piece but also become active supporters of a cause (EBB3). Participation in events and discussions geared toward raising awareness adds a layer of engagement and education, transforming the act of support into an informed and gratifying experience (EQ3), surpassing the simplicity of mere donations (EBK3).

CCC Resources Before Managing the Paradoxes

As an MIT student, Milain benefitted from the robust support network of start-up programs within the MIT ecosystem. Initially, he was awarded a fellowship from the Legatum Center at MIT, renowned for nurturing social entrepreneurship. He then enrolled in courses at D-Lab, sought guidance from MIT's Venture Mentoring Service, and attended the Martin Trust Center for MIT Entrepreneurship. This led him to participate in entrepreneurship programs such as the MIT Fuse

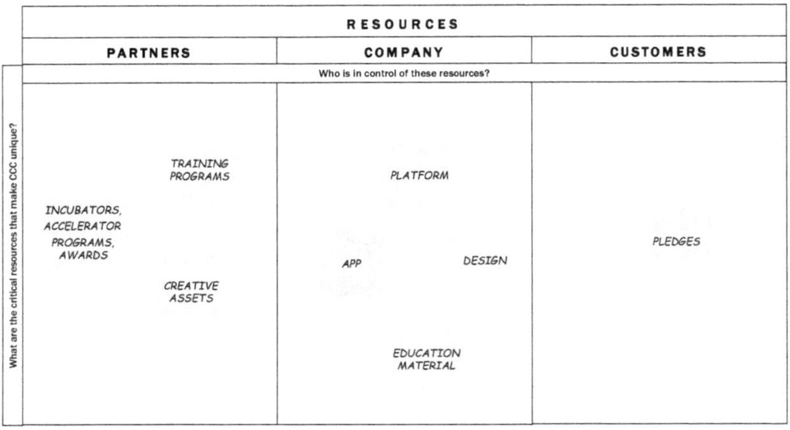

RESOURCES		
PARTNERS	**COMPANY**	**CUSTOMERS**
	Who is in control of these resources?	
TRAINING PROGRAMS	PLATFORM	
INCUBATORS, ACCELERATOR PROGRAMS, AWARDS	APP DESIGN	PLEDGES
CREATIVE ASSETS	EDUCATION MATERIAL	

(left vertical axis: What are the critical resources that make CCC unique?)

Figure 8.4 CCC Resources before managing the paradoxes

boot camp, StartMIT, and the Delta V summer accelerator, significantly enhancing his network, capabilities, knowledge, visibility, and access to funding.

Additionally, the Panzi Hospital, CCC's impact partner, was paramount in providing essential training programs, care, and psychological support to women who have survived violence in DRC. Regarding company-controlled resources, the platform is a crucial hub for product sales and customer engagement. It not only facilitates transactions but also provides avenues for education and recreational activities, such as Congo Bash parties, talks, and pop-up stores. These initiatives are designed to raise awareness about the brand and its mission. The distinctive design of CCC products is essential in seamlessly blending modern appeal with Congolese tradition and culture. This unique fusion is also fueled by the app, which empowers local women to share their creative assets, inspiring their collections.

Furthermore, CCC incorporates educational materials in various forms, including a booklet included in the shipping package, offering insight into Congo's history and its struggle with war. This educational approach aims to cultivate CCC customers as ambassadors for the company's mission. Lastly, customer engagement is a cornerstone in spreading awareness of the brand and its mission. Through the platform, individuals can fill out a form to pledge their support in ending rape in war, actively contributing to the cause (Figure 8.4).

CCC Roles Before Managing the Paradoxes

In terms of key onstage activities, effective communication of the brand and its mission is foremost. This is crucial for product differentiation and establishing a unique identity in the market. Another critical in-house activity is impact tracking, which enriches the shopping experience by giving customers meaningful insights into their contributions.

Additionally, empowering customers to pledge their support for the cause is an essential customer-driven activity that significantly contributes to raising awareness about the Congo cause. Hosting events such as talks, bash parties, and pop-up shops further strengthens the connection between customers and the culture of Congolese society, shedding light on the plight of its women.

At the backstage level, crucial activities encompass production, outsourced to trusted partner companies in Colombia. The design of collections occasionally involves partnerships with Congolese women. This is followed by the meticulous shipping and packaging preparation process, including educational materials explaining the impact of consumers' purchases. Moreover, on-field training activities for women, organized in Congo and facilitated by the Panzi Foundation, play a key role. Finally, key support activities encompass the ongoing development and maintenance of the platform and app and monitoring efforts to gauge the impact of entrepreneurial activities. This also extends to designing and implementing a robust impact-tracking system (Figure 8.5).

CCC Value Equation Before Managing the Paradoxes

The primary benefits for customers revolve around accessing uniquely styled clothing pieces. This distinctive aesthetic not only allows for a personal expression of style but also combines altruism while purchasing something they would buy anyway. Additionally, customers find value in engaging with impactful activities. The CCC reward system further enhances their experience by offering free tickets to exclusive

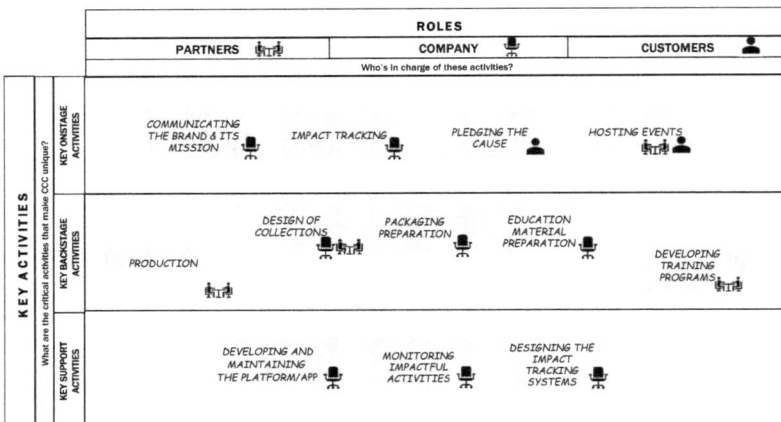

Figure 8.5 Roles before managing the paradoxes

company-organized events, expanding on the concept of impactful activities by introducing community engagement programs. Moreover, customers appreciate the ability to track the outcomes of their purchases, providing a tangible connection to the cause as well as transparency in the supply chain, demonstrating the brand's commitment to ethical and sustainable practices. CCC educational initiatives also play a crucial role in informing them about causes they may need to be better versed in. Regarding efforts, it's important to note that CCC fashion items come at a premium price point, reflecting their quality and uniqueness. While they are priced higher than items from nonconscious brands, this reflects the added value and impact of each purchase. Furthermore, CCC educational initiatives require an investment of time and attention, but they serve as an integral part of the brand's mission to raise awareness and drive meaningful change (Figure 8.6).

CCC Deals With the Paradoxes

The challenge for passionate social entrepreneurs is well-known: their noble pursuit of social goals often conflicts with the practical need to maintain financial viability. While the first year of sales was promising, a fundamental flaw in the current business model prevented Milain

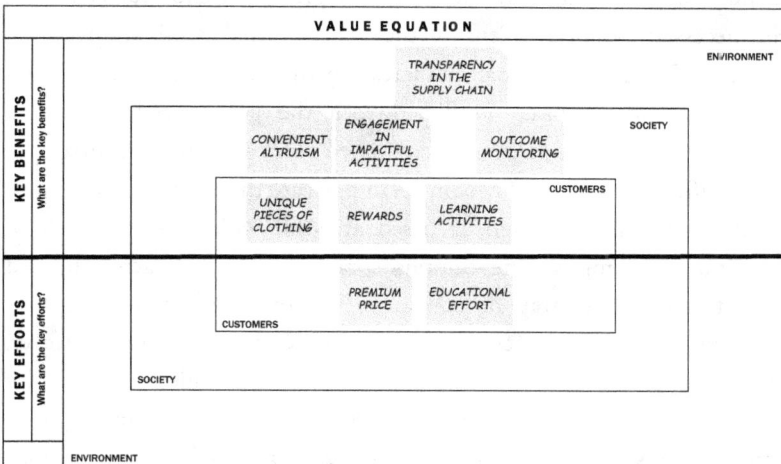

Figure 8.6 Value equation before managing the paradoxes

from achieving his vision. As a committed social entrepreneur, Milain's primary goal was to raise awareness about the violence in DRC and empower individuals to take action. To achieve this, he chose fashion as the medium to express this powerful narrative. The aspiration was for the brand to gain such recognition that wearing its clothes would become a statement in itself. However, making this vision a reality demanded a growing customer base for CCC to integrate into daily life seamlessly. This presented a significant challenge. With prices ranging from $70 for a t-shirt to around $250 for a denim jacket, the brand's positioning was beyond the reach of younger generations, especially Gen Z college students, who were a key target demographic.

Moreover, CCC collections conveyed a distinctive style deeply rooted in Congolese society and culture, making them more suitable for special occasions rather than everyday wear like work or school attire. The core issue was that, from a profit standpoint, a premium price was necessary to cover all costs associated with the product's unique identity. These costs included the training program for women survivors, community-building initiatives, educational materials for consumers, and investment in a distinctive design central to Milain's dual mission: offering something both impactful and desirable.

While reducing prices wasn't a viable option, as it would bring revenues below the threshold to attract investors, solely targeting a niche market to maintain the premium price, fell short of achieving the necessary volume to ensure the widespread dissemination of the message. So, the social goal of increasing the product's reach through a more affordable price conflicted with the profit need to keep a premium price to sustain a differentiated strategy while prioritizing a niche diffusion. What did Milain do to navigate this paradox?

As a student entrepreneur based at MIT, Milain spent much of his time on campus. The campus sprawls across 168 acres, nestled amidst a bustling array of company buildings and tech enterprises between the crowded Kendall Square and Central Square. However, amidst the crowd, one can easily identify the MIT students and faculty community by their proud display of MIT-branded attire, ranging from comfortable sweaters to iconic baseball caps and t-shirts. Institutions like MIT, alongside numerous universities and companies worldwide, utilize merchandise as a powerful means of fostering and promoting their brand identity.

This practice fosters a sense of community and belonging among students, alumni, employees, and supporters alike. Wearing or using this *swag* serves as a badge of affiliation with a particular institution or organization and the associated community. It was during this time that Milain had an epiphany: if the university and corporate swag could serve as a means for individuals to express their affiliation with a specific community, why couldn't it also be employed as a vehicle for spreading a more significant message? This insight led to Milain considering partnerships with universities and companies, wherein cobranded merchandise, distinguished by its unique designs, could transcend generic university swag, appealing to a broader audience. Pivoting to a Business to Business (B2B) market could have led to larger volumes, as businesses usually order products or services in bulk to meet their operational needs. Therefore, by collaborating with universities and companies, Milain envisioned an opportunity to not only broaden his brand's reach (and thus his message's) but also provide these organizations with a platform to invest in a social cause, aligning with their corporate social responsibility (CSR) goals. This, in turn, meant that CCC could maintain its pricing strategy, as companies would be willing to pay a premium price in exchange for the opportunity to fulfill their CSR objectives. This seemed to be a win–win situation. This intuition paved the way for a BML transformation within CCC that empowered Milain to navigate this paradox better.

CCC *After Managing the Paradoxes*

By entering into cobranded partnerships with organizations, CCC would pivot its target from conscious individual consumers to socially responsible organizations.

While individual consumers and organizations may share a common appreciation for socially impactful purchases, they are motivated by distinct factors when considering CCC products. Individual consumers

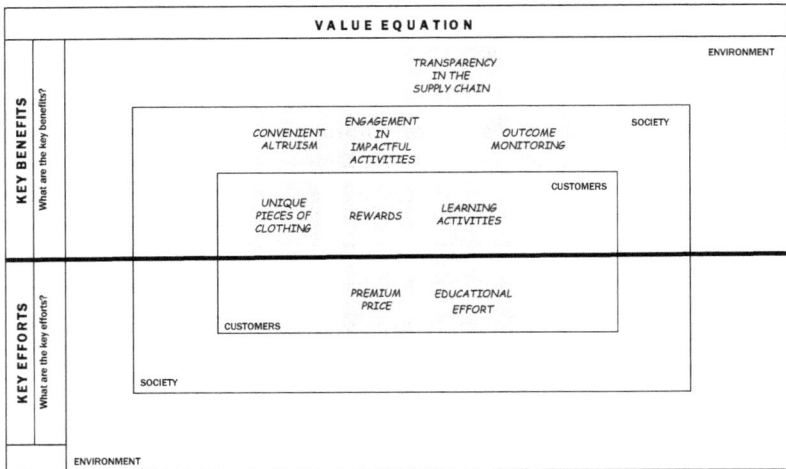

Figure 8.7 CCC BML transformation by shaping the meaning

make purchasing decisions driven by personal preferences, needs, and emotions. Conversely, in B2B markets, buying decisions are typically more complex and affected by the organization's strategic goals, constraints, and budget considerations. This underscores the need to redesign the *meaning* and find a new reason for B2B customers to love CCC.

In Chapter 1, where we explore the initiation of a BML transformation by *shaping the meaning* (the first element of the BML), you may recall that you can shape the meaning by repurposing the meaning end-use, by moving the meaning usage context, or by changing the meaning symbolic significance of the original BML.

Milain understood that, in contrast to individual consumers who purchase CCC products driven by their personal aspiration for a transition to conscious fashion and support for a specific cause, organizations would invest in CCC products for more rational and speculative purposes. These objectives may include bolstering their brand image through association with a conscious brand, championing a cause, or fulfilling CSR obligations in their annual reporting. Through applying the TST tool in analyzing this case study, we can observe Milain's initiation of his BML transformation via a shaping practice, specifically by repurposing the end-use meaning. This entails a shift in

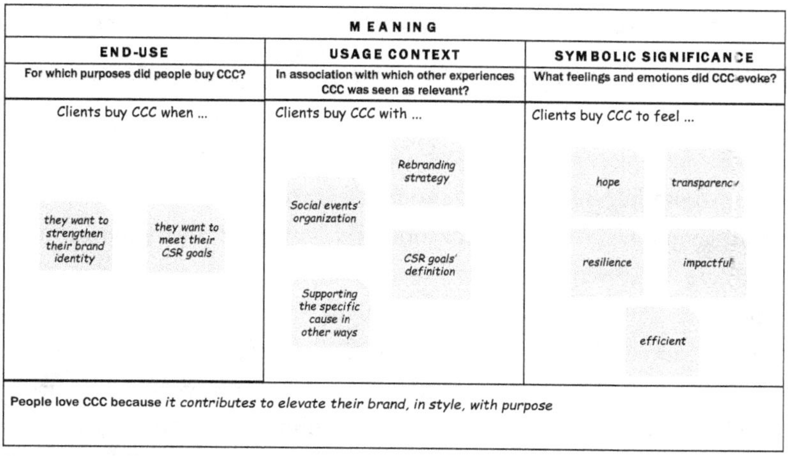

MEANING		
END-USE	**USAGE CONTEXT**	**SYMBOLIC SIGNIFICANCE**
For which purposes did people buy CCC?	In association with which other experiences CCC was seen as relevant?	What feelings and emotions did CCC evoke?
Clients buy CCC when ...	Clients buy CCC with ...	Clients buy CCC to feel ...
they want to strengthen their brand identity they want to meet their CSR goals	Rebranding strategy Social events' organization CSR goals' definition Supporting the specific cause in other ways	hope transparency resilience impactful efficient
People love CCC because *it contributes to elevate their brand, in style, with purpose*		

Figure 8.8 CCC Meaning after managing the paradoxes

the *reason why* purchasing CCC products toward the desire to *elevate their brand, in style, with purpose* (Figure 8.7).

Starting from this simple *shaping* maneuver, a whole redefinition of the *meaning* unfolds in the CCC BML. This encompasses introducing a new usage context and a new symbolic significance.

CCC Meaning After Managing the Paradoxes

The new meaning end-use encapsulates the desire to fortify the customer organization's brand identity and their commitment to achieving CSR goals through alignment with a socially conscious brand. Additionally, it involves a pledge to donate a portion of their purchases toward supporting a meaningful social cause. The new usage context extends to a spectrum of scenarios, including gifting their merchandise at social events as a token of participation, integrating it into rebranding efforts, and providing support for the same cause through alternate means such as direct donations or informative sessions. It also finds relevance within the broader scope of CSR strategy formulation. The symbolic significance is elevated by imbuing a sense of efficacy. CCC not only empowers them to effect positive change but also aids in pursuing their strategic objectives (Figure 8.8).

CCC Experiential Performance After Managing the Paradoxes

To realign the BML with the new meaning, the new EP is built on innovative EBBs. First, through a new design-as-a-service business model, customers not only cobrand but also codesign merchandise in collaboration with organizations. The entire process is efficiently managed online, where organizations can complete an online form to articulate their requirements, encompassing item types, design concepts, brand identity, customization preferences, and desired quantities. Thanks to their AI models, CCC can quickly propose design ideas for online discussion between customers and CCC's creative team, ensuring a seamless realization of the customer's vision and eliminating design-related challenges. This leads to a more cooperative, streamlined, and tailored experience, surpassing in-house options and partnerships with white-label/labeled fashion brands.

Furthermore, CCC's emphasis on high-quality, sustainable materials and meticulous design allows customers to deliver premium merchandise, debunking the notion that merchandise is limited to basic items akin to sleepwear. Secondly, the option for customers to place merchandise orders directly on the CCC platform translates to a swifter experience, with reduced lead times ranging from two to four weeks. It's

EXPERIENTIAL PERFORMANCE		
EXPERIENTIAL BUILDING BLOCKS (EBB)	EXPERIENTIAL QUALITY (EQ)	EXPERIENTIAL BENCHMARK (EBK)
What are the relevant aspects of the customer experience?	In which way do these aspects create more value?	Compared to what substitute/similar experiences?
With *CCC* the user can	How?	Differently from ....
EBB.1	In a more COLLABORATIVE way	IN-HOUSE OPTIONS
DESIGN THEIR MERCHANDISE	In an EASIER way	
	In a more EFFICIENT way	WHITE LABEL/LABELLED FASHION BRANDS
	In a more CUSTOM way	
EBB.2	In a more PREMIUM way	
ORDER/PURCHASE THEIR MERCH	In a FASTER way	WHITE LABEL/LABELLED FASHION BRANDS
	In a more CONVENIENT way	
	In a more IMPACTFUL way	
EBB.3		
SUPPORT A CAUSE	In a more CONVENIENT way	DONATIONS
	In a more COMMUNICATIVE way	

Figure 8.9 CCC Experiential performance after managing the paradoxes

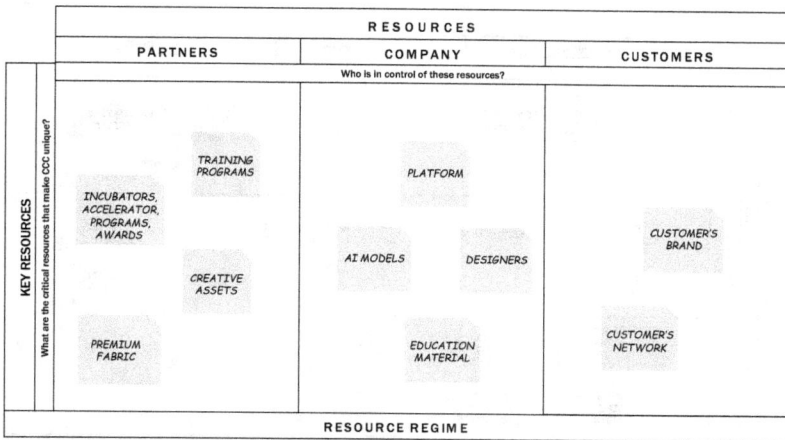

RESOURCES		
PARTNERS	**COMPANY**	**CUSTOMERS**
	Who is in control of these resources?	

Figure layout (Key Resources / What are the critical resources that make CCC unique?):

- INCUBATORS, ACCELERATOR, PROGRAMS, AWARDS
- TRAINING PROGRAMS
- PLATFORM
- CREATIVE ASSETS
- AI MODELS
- DESIGNERS
- CUSTOMER'S BRAND
- PREMIUM FABRIC
- EDUCATION MATERIAL
- CUSTOMER'S NETWORK

RESOURCE REGIME

Figure 8.10 CCC Resources after managing the paradoxes

also more convenient, as the minimum order quantities (MOQs) are lower than industry standards. Most notably, each purchase contributes to upskilling women in Congo, aligning with customers' environmental, social, and governance (ESG) and diversity, equity, and inclusion (DEI) goals. Finally, supporting a cause is made more accessible compared to conventional donation methods. This is thanks to exchanging premium merchandise materials, allowing organizations to achieve impact and marketing objectives concurrently. The communication aspect is enhanced, as each piece of merchandise comes with labels explaining the specific type of impact that each purchase has in terms of training days (Figure 8.9).

CCC Resources After Managing the Paradoxes

As a result of this realignment, there will be a notable shift in the resource regime. The new BML platform takes on an even more central role, serving as the conduit for codesigning, interacting with clients, and effectively conveying the brand's mission. One of the major distinctions from the previous BML system lies in incorporating AI models trained on authentic artwork. This is pivotal in enabling CCC to outperform competitors in terms of design speed and content originality. Furthermore, the team of designers plays a crucial role in tailoring designs

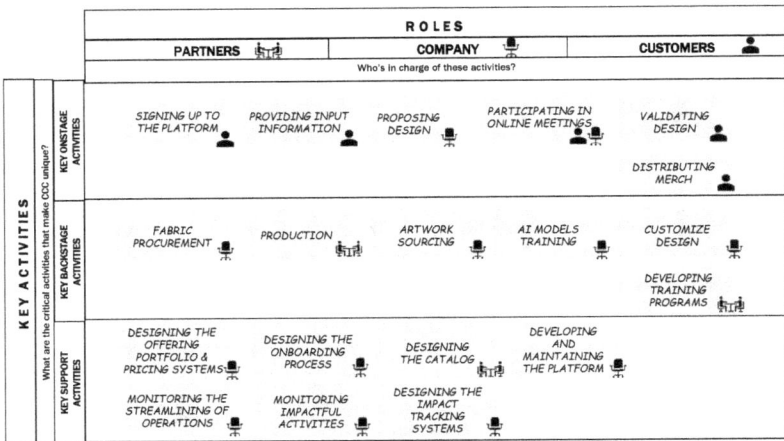

Figure 8.11 CCC Roles after managing the paradoxes

to align with customers' unique visions, ensuring the merchandise stands out. Lastly, the cobranding approach places great importance on customer brands, not only for increasing CCC's reputation but also for extending the reach of the CCC message across a wider network (Figure 8.10).

CCC Roles After Managing the Paradoxes

In the newly configured BML model, customer-driven onstage activities encompass signing up on the platform, providing input through online forms, engaging in virtual meetings with CCC designers to discuss ideas, validating designs, and ultimately distributing the merchandise to amplify CCC's reach. At this onstage level, the company proposes designs to customers based on their input from the online form. Simultaneously, at the backstage level, the company oversees critical operations such as fabric procurement, ensuring premium quality merchandise that harmonizes style with social impact. This also involves managing artwork sourcing and training AI models to enhance service efficiency. Additionally, there's a focus on customizing designs in alignment with customer visions and brand identities.

Production activities and the development of training programs for women survivors fall under the responsibility of CCC partners.

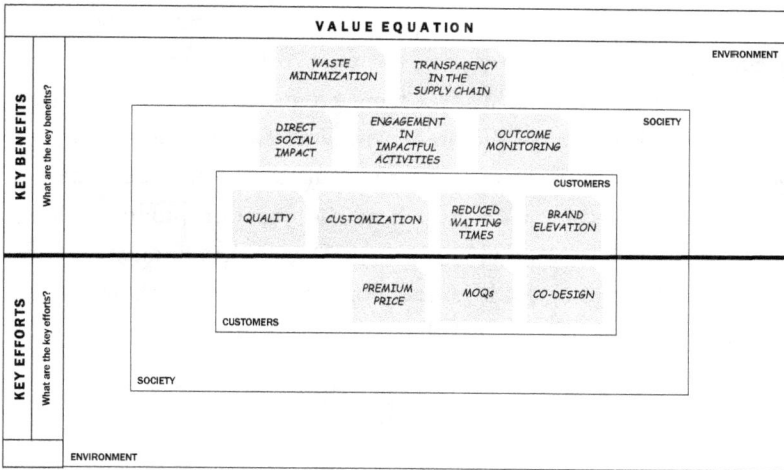

Figure 8.12 Value equation after managing the paradoxes

Meanwhile, support activities encompass designing the offering portfolio and pricing systems, crafting an engaging onboarding process, creating a compelling catalog to effectively communicate CCC offerings to customers, platform development and maintenance, and the vigilant monitoring of streamlined operations and impactful activities. This includes the design and implementation of an impact tracking system (Figure 8.11).

CCC Value Equation After Managing the Paradoxes

In the new value equation, primary benefits from a customer's perspective encompass enhanced product quality, a stylish design, customization aligned with their brand identity, the social impact of their purchase, and the elevated brand visibility gained through using the merchandise as a marketing tool for the brand's engagement in social initiatives. Additionally, technical advantages include reduced service waiting times and lower MOQs compared to industry standards. Moreover, customers benefit from technical advantages, such as reduced service waiting times and notably lower MOQs compared to industry standards. Beyond the immediate customer experience, these aspects contribute significantly to sustainable production practices by minimizing waste. Furthermore, customer engagement in the design process represents an opportunity not only to enhance the customization aspect but also to cultivate a more profound connection with the brand and instill a sense of shared ownership. However, it's essential to acknowledge the corresponding efforts required. This includes premium pricing, which is in place to reflect the superior product quality. Additionally, while minimum orders are lower than industry norms, they are still necessary. An investment of time and effort is also required for active participation in the design process (Figure 8.12).

So What?

The story of CCC illustrates the power of adopting a forward-thinking mindset to navigate the conflict between two seemingly opposing goals. Milain's determination to pursue a both/and leadership harnessed creativity to reconcile the divide between profit growth and social impact. In the face of fluctuating capital flows from the B2C market, which suggested lowering prices and compromising on quality to expand the brand's reach, he chose a different path. Instead of yielding to convention, he embraced change with an open mind. He identified the most polarized element in his BML that leaned heavily toward the social goal (i.e., meaning) and started a transformation right from there (BML transformation by shaping the meaning). This shift led him into a new market, where he had to redefine his competitive advantage without compromising his mission to impact the world positively. This exemplifies what we mean by embracing TST. Milain's journey underscores the complexity of managerial decision making in the face of paradoxes and the importance of adopting a TST approach to embrace and leverage conflicting goals for long-term success.

Chapter Overview

This chapter presents the last of our key challenges: paradox management. In business leadership, a paradox represents a set of objectives or challenges that may appear incompatible, leading to a perceived either/or choice. These paradoxes include dilemmas such as managing change while maintaining stability, balancing local market adaptation with a standardized global approach, and reconciling cost reduction with quality improvement.

Conventional either/or thinking falls short in today's complex business landscape. The theory of paradox management emphasizes the need to leverage both ends of each paradox for effective leadership and decision making. Paradoxical leadership departs from stability and predictability, thriving on dynamism and change. It promotes a culture of experimentation, learning from failures, and continuous adaptation. The TST tool can help cultivate this mindset. It trains entrepreneurs and managers to navigate paradoxes creatively. The tool serves a dual purpose: first, it aids in understanding current business assumptions and identifying polarizations; second, it provides a framework to experiment with new alternative business model logics using polarizations as a starting point. The chapter concludes with an analysis of the CCC, underscoring the strategic significance of adopting a TST approach.

Conclusions

In this book, we aim to guide you through the complex landscape of business model transformation by offering actionable tools and real-world examples drawn from our observations of both the successes and setbacks of companies on this journey—insights that we've shared throughout the book.

Throughout the exploration of various cases, we highlight the significant impact of a lack of creative thinking, especially when navigating external changes. For example, during the global pandemic, businesses that relied solely on physical presence struggled, while those with digital strategies thrived. Similarly, as discussed in Chapter 7, the rise of Artificial Intelligence (AI) introduced market disruptions across industries.

Competitiveness Beyond Products

The book emphasizes a shift in the concept of competitiveness. The traditional focus on having the best product or service is diminishing. Now, the core of competitiveness lies in the innovative capabilities embedded within the business model.

Thriving Through Transformation

Success increasingly depends on the willingness to confront and reshape existing business models. Companies that embrace innovation or undergo radical transformation are better positioned to turn threats into opportunities.

Understanding Assumptions for Change

Examining and questioning the foundational assumptions of current business models is crucial. Challenging these assumptions is key to driving effective change and adaptation.

Elemental Transformation

The book introduces the concept of elemental transformation, suggesting that each dimension (and sub-dimension) within the business model logic can serve as a catalyst for a holistic evolution of the business model.

Building on these key takeaways, the book aims to provide a comprehensive framework that seamlessly integrates two interdependent goals:

Goal 1: Understanding Assumptions Behind a Business Model

With the TST tool, the analysis of the BML's main elements responds to the need to uncover the foundational assumptions upon which companies build their business models. It also serves as a diagnostic tool to unearth outdated assumptions and pave the way for strategic renewal.

Analyzing into the *Meaning* facilitates a deeper understanding of the assumptions regarding why individuals opt for a particular value proposition. Simultaneously, scrutinizing the *EP* provides insights into how the configuration of customer experience contributes more value compared to both direct and indirect competitors. The exploration of *Resources* provides valuable insights into assumptions about the pivotal tangible or intangible assets crucial for value creation and identifies those who wield control over them. Similarly, mapping the *Roles* enables contemplation on the essential activities within our business models, their flow, and the individuals accountable for them. Lastly, dissecting the *Value Equation* aids in clarifying assumptions about how customers perceive value. This involves identifying the benefits and efforts associated with acquiring the offered value, providing a comprehensive understanding of the customer's perspective.

Goal 2: Experiment with Alternative Business Model Logic Transformations

The second goal is to stimulate creativity and—for example—expand the mental horizons of decision makers entrenched in past successes and traditional business planning methodologies. Given the dynamic nature of industries and the potential emergence of disruptive events, fostering creativity becomes paramount. This is particularly crucial when managing external changes induced by rapid innovation, unforeseen events, or the juggling of conflicting strategic goals. In such scenarios, creativity plays a pivotal role in turning threats into opportunities for transformative change. We strongly believe that creativity can be cultivated like any other skill. Hence, the TST tool introduces five transformative practices (*shaping, stretching, sharing, switching,* and *swapping*) as a structured framework to brainstorm ideas for innovating the BML. This approach focuses on leveraging one element at a time and acknowledges the "domino effect" that results from the consequential realignment of the remaining elements to the new one. This micro-perspective can be really powerful in expanding individuals' creativity horizons. Yet, to fully unlock this creative potential (Goal 2), it's essential to properly acknowledge the assumptions behind the as-is BML (Goal 1).

When Should You Use the TST Tool?

The TST tool focuses on those elements of the business model that capture critical assumptions about value creation. Its level of abstraction on five dimensions is meant to foster shared understanding and facilitate an agile process of experimentation. The TST tool finds its strength in the realm of idea generation, serving as a valuable asset during brainstorming sessions for innovating a company's business model or initiating a new project. It can also be integrated with other tools to support the more specific adaptation of the business model with regard to financial, organizational and management aspects. In general, the tool can be used in different use cases, here's the most common ones.

Business Model Diagnosis

The TST tool can be used to analyze and identify outdated assumptions in the BML, potentially requiring user and market research for deeper insights. It can also be used to rank the weakest BML elements based on their relevance and innovation potential.

Generation and Selection of Alternative Business Model Scenarios

The most vulnerable BML elements can be used as a starting point to select alternative transformational practices and put them into action. The realignment of all the other elements with each transformation will ensure overall consistency. Repeating this process for various elements makes it possible to craft alternative BML innovation scenarios. The integration of design thinking prioritization tools (such as dot voting or assumption mapping) can be useful to compare the different BML innovation scenarios and select the most viable ones.

Business Model Validation

The TST tool can be used to assess the various feedback following a first experiment iteration, allowing for refinement and decision making regarding further investment or disengagement. It can be used as an integration of other business model visual tools to zoom into specific aspects of the business model and its value proposition.

It's essential to note that the book's frameworks aim to stimulate creative thinking and don't prescribe specific guidelines for decision making,

In essence, this book serves as a guide based on real-world observations and experiences. It underscores the pivotal role of business models in determining competitiveness, emphasizing the need for continuous adaptation and innovation. The insights derived from this exploration are intended to empower readers to successfully navigate the intricate dynamics of business model transformation.

Bibliography

Chapter 1

Alexis, C. 2022. "The Symbolic Life of the Moleskine Notebook." In *The Material Culture of Writing*, 25.

Lojacono, G. and G. Zaccai. 2004. "The Evolution of the Design-Inspired Enterprise." *MIT Sloan Management Review*.

Tuci, M. 2020. *The Role of Lovemarks From an Experience Marketing Perspective: The Case of Moleskine*.

Verganti, R. 2008. "Design, Meanings, and Radical Innovation: A Metamodel and a Research Agenda." *Journal of Product Innovation Management* 25, no. 5, pp. 436–456.

Verganti, R. 2018. *Overcrowded. Designing Meaningful Products in a World Awash With Ideas*. Project Manager (IL).

Wilson, E.J. 2005. "The Nose Knows: New Product Development at Yankee Candle Company." *Journal of Business Research* 58, no. 7, pp. 989–994.

Yalom, I.D. 2012. *Love's Executioner: And Other Tales of Psychotherapy*. Basic Books.

Chapter 2

Da Silva, E.C. 2021. "Customer Experience Project: A Framework to Create and Deliver Value to Customers." *International Journal of Marketing Studies* 13, no. 3, p. 1–21.

Girija, S. and D.R. Sharma. 2021. "Customer Experience by Design or by Accident." In *Crafting Customer Experience Strategy*, 117–128. Emerald Publishing Limited.

Michelli, J.A. and D. Hill. 2007. *The Starbucks Experience*. AML/McGraw-Hill Audio.

Povoledo, E. 2018. "Does Italy Want More Cafes? Starbucks Hopes So." *The New York Times*, A6-L.

Quartier, K., A. Petermans, T.C. Melewar, C. Dennis. 2021. *The Value of Design in Retail and Branding*. Regno Unito: Emerald Publishing Limited.

Rawson, A., E. Duncan, and C. Jones. 2013. "The Truth About Customer Experience." *Harvard Business Review* 91, no. 9, p. 90–98.

Sinek, S. 2009. "Start With Why: How Great Leaders Inspire Everyone to Take Action." Regno Unito: Penguin Publishing Group.

Chapter 3

Ahlstrand, B., J. Lampel, and H. Mintzberg. 2001. *Strategy Safari: A Guided Tour Through the Wilds of Strategic Management*. Simon and Schuster.

Centobelli, P., R. Cerchione, E. Esposito, and M. Raffa. 2016. "The Revolution of Crowdfunding in Social Knowledge Economy: Literature Review and Identification of Business Models." *Advanced Science Letters* 22, no. 5–6, pp. 1666–1669.

Kraaijenbrink, J., J.C. Spender, and A.J. Groen. 2010. "The Resource-Based View: A Review and Assessment of Its Critiques." *Journal of Management* 36, no. 1, pp. 349–372.

Lockett, A. and S. Thompson. 2004. "Edith Penrose's Contributions to the Resource-Based View: An Alternative Perspective." *Journal of Management Studies* 41, no. 1, pp. 193–203.

Penrose, E.T. 2009. *The Theory of the Growth of the Firm*. Regno Unito: Oxford University Press.

Rougès, J.F. and B. Montreuil. May 2014. "Crowdsourcing Delivery: New Interconnected Business Models to Reinvent Delivery." In 1st International Physical Internet Conference 1 vols, 1–19. Québec City (Canada) IPIC.

Teece, D.J. 2008. *Technological Know-how, Organizational Capabilities, and Strategic Management: Business Strategy and Enterprise Development in Competitive Environments*. Singapore. World Scientific Publishing Company.

Tripp, J., D. H. McKnight, and N. Lankton. 2022. "What Most Influences Consumers' Intention to Use? Different Motivation and Trust Stories for Uber, Airbnb, and Taskrabbit." *European Journal of Information Systems*, pp. 1–23.

Venkatesan, R. and S. Gibbs, Shea and D. Shively. "Netflix, Inc.: The Mouse Strikes Back. Darden Case No. UVA-M-0975." Available at SSRN: https://ssrn.com/abstract=3703310 or http://dx.doi.org/10.2139/ssrn.3703310

Vertesi, J.A., A. Goldstein, D. Enriquez, L. Liu, and K.T. Miller. 2020. "Pre-Automation: Insourcing and Automating the Gig Economy." *Sociologica* 14, no. 3, pp. 167–193.

Chapter 4

Acquier, A., V. Carbone, and D. Massé. 2019. "How to Create Value (s) in the Sharing Economy: Business Models, Scalability, and Sustainability." *Technology Innovation Management Review* 9, no. 2.

De Angelis, R. 2018. *Business Models in the Circular Economy: Concepts, Examples and Theory*. Springer.

Osterwalder, A., Y. Pigneur, and C.L. Tucci. 2005. "Clarifying Business Models: Origins, Present, and Future of the Concept." *Communications of the Association for Information Systems* 16, no. 1, p. 1.

Osterwalder, A. and Y. Pigneur. 2013. *Business Model Generation: A Handbook for Visionaries, Game Changers, and Challengers.* Germania, Wiley.

Porter, M.E. 1985. "Technology and Competitive Advantage." *Journal of Business Strategy* 5, no. 3, pp. 60–78.

Porter, M.E. 2001. "The Value Chain and Competitive Advantage." *Understanding Business Processes* 2, pp. 50–66.

Zamora, E.A. 2016. "Value Chain Analysis: A Brief Review." *Asian Journal of Innovation and Policy* 5, no. 2, pp. 116–128.

Chapter 5

Aversa, P., A. Hervas-Drane, and M. Evenou. 2019. "Business Model Responses to Digital Piracy." *California Management Review* 61, no. 2, pp. 30–58.

Blois, K. 2004. "Analyzing Exchanges Through the Use of Value Equations." *Journal of Business & Industrial Marketing* 19, no. 4, pp. 250–257.

Braun, M., S. Latham, and B. Cannatelli. 2019. "Strategy and Business Models: Why Winning Companies Need Both." *Journal of Business Strategy* 40, no. 5, pp, 39–45.

Brem, A., M. Maier, and C. Wimschneider. 2016. "Competitive Advantage Through Innovation: The Case of Nespresso." *European Journal of Innovation Management* 19, no. 1, pp. 133–148.

Dragomir, V.D. and M. Dumitru. 2022. "Practical Solutions for Circular Business Models in the Fashion Industry." *Cleaner Logistics and Supply Chain* 4, p. 100040.

Green, P.E., Y. Wind, and A.K. Jain. 2000. "Benefit Bundle Analysis." *Journal of Advertising Research* 40, no. 6, pp. 32–37.

Hvass, K.K. 2022. "Business Model Innovation Through Second Hand Retailing: A Fashion Industry Case." In *New Business Models for Sustainable Fashion,* 11–32. Routledge.

Ibid.

Matzler, K., F. Bailom, S.F. von den Eichen, and T. Kohler. 2013. "Business Model Innovation: Coffee Triumphs for Nespresso." *Journal of Business Strategy* 34, no. 2, pp. 30–37.

Osterwalder, A., Y. Pigneur, G. Bernarda, and A. Smith. 2015. *Value Proposition Design: How to Create Products and Services Customers Want,* 2 vols. John Wiley & Sons.

Trabucchi, D., L. Talenti, and T. Buganza. 2019. "How Do Big Bang Disruptors Look Like? A Business Model Perspective." *Technological Forecasting and Social Change* 141, pp. 330–340.

Chapter 6

Christensen, C.M. 2013. "The Innovator's Dilemma: When New Technologies Cause Great Firms to Fail." *Harvard Business Review Press.*
Christensen, C.M., M.E. Raynor, and S.D. Anthony. 2003. *Six Keys to Building New Markets by Unleashing Disruptive Innovation.* Harvard Management. EEUU.
Christensen, C.M. 1997. *The Innovator's Dilemma.* Harvard Business School Press, Cambridge, Mass.
Downes, L. and P. Nunes. 2013. *Blockbuster Becomes a Casualty of Big Bang Disruption.* Harvard Business Review, 7 vols.
O'Reilly, C. and A.J. Binns. 2019. "The Three Stages of Disruptive Innovation: Idea Generation, Incubation, and Scaling." *California Management Review* 61, no. 3, pp. 49–71.
Păvăloaia, V.D. and S.C. Necula. 2023. "Artificial Intelligence as a Disruptive Technology—A Systematic Literature Review." *Electronics* 12, no. 5, p. 110.
Vlaskovits, P. 2011. "Henry Ford, Innovation, and That 'Faster Horse' Quote." Harvard Business Review 29, no. 08.

Chapter 7

"Binance Is Strongly Leaning Toward Scrapping FTX Rescue Takeover After First Glance at Books: Source." n.d. CoinDesk. www.coindesk. com/business/2022/11/09/binance-is-strongly-leaning-toward -scrapping-ftx-rescue-takeover-after-first-glance-at-books-source/#:~: text=CoinDesk%20reports%20that%20cryptocurrency%20exchange, person%20familiar%20with%20the%20matter.
"Bitcoin, Ethereum Plummet as Crypto Market Falls Below $1 Trillion Overnight." n.d. Decrypt. https://decrypt.co/113996/bitcoin-ethereum- plummet-crypto-market-falls-below-1-trillion-overnight.
"California Financial Regulator Announces FTX Investigation." n.d. CoinDesk. www.coindesk.com/policy/2022/11/10/california-financial-regulator- announces-ftx-investigation/.
"Divisions in Sam Bankman-Fried's Crypto Empire Blur on His Trading Titan Alameda's Balance Sheet." n.d. CoinDesk. www.coindesk.com/ business/2022/11/02/divisions-in-sam-bankman-frieds-crypto-empire- blur-on-his-trading-titan-alamedas-balance-sheet/.

Bloomberg. n.d. "Binance to Sell $529 Million of Bankman-Fried's FTT Token." www.bloomberg.com/news/articles/2022-11-06/binance-to-sell-529-million-of-ftt-token-amids-revelations.

Cliffe, S. 2001. "What a Star-What a Jerk." *Harvard Business Review* 79, no. 8, pp. 37–48.

Jalan, A. and R. Matkovskyy. 2023. "Systemic Risks in the Cryptocurrency Market: Evidence From the FTX Collapse." *Finance Research Letters* 53, p. 103670.

Reuters. n.d. "Crypto Exchange FTX Saw $6 Bln in Withdrawals in 72 Hours." www.reuters.com/business/finance/crypto-exchange-ftx-saw-6-bln-withdrawals-72-hours-ceo-message-staff-2022-11-08/#:~:text=Nov%20 8%20(Reuters)%20%2D%20Crypto,that%20was%20seen%20by%20 Reuters.

Rigby, D.K., S. Elk, and S. Berez. 2020. "Develop Agility That Outlasts the Pandemic." *Harvard Business Review*.

Taleb, N.N. 2010. *The Black Swan: Second Edition: The Impact of the Highly Improbable Fragility*. Stati Uniti: Random House Publishing Group.

Taleb, N.N. 2012. *Antifragile: Things That Gain From Disorder*. Regno Unito: Random House Publishing Group.

Chapter 8

Gaim, M., S. Clegg, and M.P.E. Cunha. 2021. "Managing Impressions Rather Than Emissions: Volkswagen and The False Mastery of Paradox." *Organization Studies* 42, no. 6, pp. 949–970.

Johansen, J.H. 2018. *Paradox Management: Contradictions and Tensions in Complex Organizations*. Springer.

Johnson, B. 2014. "Reflections: A Perspective on Paradox and Its Application to Modern Management." *The Journal of Applied Behavioral Science* 50, no. 2, pp. 206–212.

Lewis, M.W. 2000. "Exploring Paradox: Toward a More Comprehensive Guide." *Academy of Management Review* 25, no. 4, pp. 760–776.

Smith, W.K. and M.W. Lewis. 2011. "Toward a Theory of Paradox: A Dynamic Equilibrium Model of Organizing." *Academy of Management Review* 36, no. 2, pp. 381–403.

Smith, W.K., M.W. Lewis, and M.L. Tushman. 2016. "Both/and Leadership." *Harvard Business Review* 94, no. 5, pp. 62–70.

Sundaramurthy, C. and M. Lewis. 2003. "Control and Collaboration: Paradoxes of Governance." *Academy of Management Review* 28, no. 3, pp. 397–415.

Waldman, D.A. and D.E. Bowen. 2016. "Learning to Be a Paradox-Savvy Leader." *Academy of Management Perspectives* 30, no. 3, pp. 316–327.

Links:

https://franchiseexecutives.com.au/mcdonalds-celebrates-30-years-of-
    mccafe/

https://news.mit.edu/2022/bringing-hope-transformation-congo-milain-
    fayulu-0524

Index

About the Authors

Michele Simoni is full professor of Innovation and Business Design at the University of Naples Parthenope. He is the director of the PhD in Entrepreneurship and Innovation jointly held by the University of Campania Vanvitelli and Parthenope University. He is currently the coordinator of the Observatory on Local Innovation Systems (SLIOB), created in 2018 by DISAQ as part of its Department of Excellence project funded by MIUR.

He's a member of the executive committee of the Master's program in Entrepreneurship and Innovation Management (MEIM), launched in 2022 by Parthenope University in collaboration with the Sloan School of Management of the Massachusetts Institute of Technology (MIT).

He sits on the scientific committee of the VIMASS, a research lab devoted to innovation in the health care sector. He participates in the faculty of Fintech Lab Naples, dedicated to promoting open innovation in the Fintech sector.

He has been coordinator of the theme division on Technology and Innovation Marketing of the Italian Marketing Scientific Society (Società Italiana di Marketing—SIM).

He is a member of the editorial board of the *Italian Journal of Marketing*, the official academic journal of SIM, and the *Journal of Innovation Economics and Management*. He also serves as associate guest editor and ad hoc reviewer for several leading scholarly journals.

His research focuses on how complexity affects innovation and value-creation processes. In particular, he studies how the interplay between external and internal complexity affects technological and design innovation in entrepreneurial and managerial organizations and ecosystems. He adopts different research methodologies: case study, quantitative statistical analysis, and agent-based simulation models.

He is the author of several books and articles published in leading international journals.

Eva Panetti is Assistant Professor at the School of Management Fribourg (HEG-FR) at the University of Applied Sciences and Arts of Western Switzerland (HES-SO). Until 2024, she served as Assistant Professor of Innovation and Business Design and Business Planning at the Parthenope University of Naples (Italy) and Adjunct professor at Vilnius University, teaching Strategic Management. Eva's expertise extends to her role as a design coach at Parthenope University's "Fintech Lab," where she guided master's students and practitioners in crafting innovative fintech solutions for banks and companies in the insurance industry. She has also provided advisory services to companies in the publishing and insurance sectors, assisting them in redefining their business models. Her research interests revolve around business model innovations, entrepreneurship, and innovation ecosystems. Eva has combined her academic work with initiatives aimed at supporting regional entrepreneurial ecosystems. Her contributions include involvement in projects such as the MIT Sloan Regional Entrepreneurship Acceleration Program (REAP) and the MIT Sloan Global Program with Parthenope University. She also conducted research at the MIT Industrial Performance Center. In 2020, she received the Guido Dorso Prize for her commitment to Innovation and Entrepreneurship in the Campania Region (Italy), awarded by the Senate of the Italian Republic. Eva also played a key role in establishing the UNESCO Chair on "Entrepreneurship and Innovation Lifelong Learning in Business Ecosystems of Mediterranean and MENA countries," awarded to Parthenope University in 2021. She has authored numerous publications in leading international journals and is the author of the book *The Dynamics of Local Innovation Systems* (2019), published by Routledge.

Marco Ferretti is full professor of Entrepreneurship and Innovation at the Parthenope University of Naples where he has served as a member of the Board of Directors. He is also responsible for the "Department of Excellence" project with a budget of €6.5ML and champion of the newly established UNESCO Chair "Entrepreneurship and lifelong learning innovation in the business ecosystems of MENA countries." In 2020, the Minister of University and Research appointed him as the national coordinator for preparing the section dedicated to the blue economy in the National Research Program 2020–2027.

He has a degree in Economics from the University of Naples, an MBA from the Sloan School of Management of the Massachusetts Institute of Technology, and a PhD in Engineering from the University of Padua.

His research interests focus on the topics of strategy, innovation, and entrepreneurship and has a long-standing experience in building and accelerating start-ups. He is the author of over 90 articles published in authoritative Italian and foreign scientific journals.

www.ingramcontent.com/pod-product-compliance
Lightning Source LLC
Chambersburg PA
CBHW061220220326
41599CB00025B/4700